C000132822

PROVOCATIONS

THE PRESS
FREEDOM MYTH

JONATHAN HEAWOOD

SERIES EDITOR:

YASMIN ALIBHAI-BROWN

Biteback Publishing

First published in Great Britain in 2019 by
Biteback Publishing Ltd
Westminster Tower
3 Albert Embankment
London SE1 7SP
Copyright © Jonathan Heawood 2019

ISBN 978-1-78590-544-5

10 9 8 7 6 5 4 3 2 1

A CIP catalogue record for this book is available from the British Library.

Set in Stempel Garamond

Printed and bound in Great Britain by
CPI Group (UK) Ltd, Croydon CR0 4YY

MIX
Paper from
responsible sources
FSC
www.fsc.org
FSC® C020471

*This book is dedicated to my family,
with love and thanks.*

Contents

Preface

I USED TO HAVE complete faith. Not in God or the afterlife or anything incredible like that, but in the concept of press freedom. For a long time, it was the closest thing I had to a religion.

I worked as a journalist and then as a press freedom campaigner. I defended the rights of reporters around the world who were imprisoned, tortured or killed for doing their jobs. I protested outside embassies, lobbied Parliaments and called for new laws to protect the freedom of the press.

To me, journalists were the good guys and anyone who wanted to silence them was the enemy. I saw what happened when well-meaning laws were used to stifle reporters, and I agreed with Thomas Jefferson that 'our liberty depends on the freedom of the press, and that cannot be limited without being lost'. If you chip away at press freedom, I thought, you take power away from journalists and put it in the hands of the authorities. At least, that was what I told myself.

I tried to ignore the critics of the press, who pointed out that some newspapers are a tissue of lies and distortions. *So what if the press is biased?* I retorted. *The whole point of press freedom is to provide a range of viewpoints. If you don't like right-wing papers, read left-wing ones. If you don't like celebrity journalism, ignore it. So what if journalists sometimes get their facts wrong? You don't want the state telling you what to believe, do you? You think that reporters are poking their noses into people's private lives? Well, if you've got nothing to hide, you've got nothing to fear.*

My faith in press freedom took a knock in 2011, when it came out that journalists at the *News of the World* newspaper had hacked into the phone messages of a murdered schoolgirl called Milly Dowler. She was neither a celebrity nor a politician, but a child who had suffered the worst fate imaginable. My doubts grew over the following year, as the Leveson Inquiry into phone hacking exposed more and more abuses of power by a range of national newspapers. I became actively suspicious as those same newspapers fought tooth and nail against Leveson's recommendations, accusing him of bringing about 'the death of press freedom' or damaging the public's 'right to know'.

I had spent years campaigning for press freedom, and I did not believe that Leveson's proposals for enhanced regulation would stop editors from holding the powerful to account or exposing corruption. I began to wonder about press freedom. Was this principle really being used to protect the public from an overmighty state? Or had it been co-opted by powerful businessmen to protect themselves from scrutiny? I started to agree with Mark Twain that, whilst there are laws to protect the freedom of the press, 'there are none that are worth anything to protect the people from the press'.

But when I shared my concerns with friends in the industry, they were appalled. 'I thought you were one of us,' said one former colleague in a tone of regret. I thought I still was. I certainly still believed that journalists should be free to inform their communities, represent the public and speak truth to power. But I did not believe that they should be free to knowingly lie or destroy people's private lives or incite hatred against vulnerable groups.

I tried to explain to my old friends that they were wrong; that there was nothing to fear from Leveson; and that there must be a way to drive up standards of journalism whilst protecting the freedom of the press. But I found it difficult to talk about this when they were so fundamentalist in their views. For them, any form of regulation was anathema. They believed that society benefited from an absolutely free press – despite the evidence that some newspapers had systematically abused that freedom. After a while, I gave up on these conversations. I respected the integrity of my friends' position, but I thought that they were wrong.

And so I was surprised when they began to change their tune on regulation. The same editors, reporters and newspaper owners who had been noisily opposed to the regulation of newspapers began calling for the regulation of social media. All of a sudden, these hardened advocates of media freedom were appalled by the horrors that were cropping up on platforms like Facebook, Twitter and YouTube. *Fake news! Hate speech!*

Invasions of privacy! In their excitement, they seemed to forget their own track record in these areas. They also seemed to forget their commitment to media freedom.

Until very recently, the press justified fake news as the hallmark of a free media. *What, would you have a Ministry of Truth?* they demanded whenever anyone called for newspapers to be regulated. Now, they were describing fake news as a threat to democracy, and calling on the government to do something about it.

I was confused. Hadn't Thomas Jefferson been right to say that if you limit press freedom, you lose it? If so, why did these newspapers want to limit the freedom of social media companies and their users? Don't social media platforms have the same rights as traditional newspapers and broadcasters? After all, Facebook, Twitter and YouTube can be powerful tools for social change. They, too, can host content that holds the powerful to account and exposes wrongdoing. If the regulation of newspapers is dangerous, then the regulation of social media must be at least as dangerous – if not more so, because it could affect what we all say to each other as individuals.

What is the difference between regulation of the press

and regulation of social media? The cynical answer is that press regulation would damage the business models of some newspapers, whilst social media regulation would protect those same newspapers from competition. Effective regulation of social media would stop platforms from promoting fake news and hate speech and invading people's privacy – whilst an unregulated press would remain free to do all of those things and more. Social media regulation would allow newspapers to get back to business as usual, whilst press regulation would force them to raise their game.

Am I right to be cynical? Is 'press freedom' just a story that newspapers use to protect their business interests? A fairy tale? If so, should we abandon press freedom, as we have abandoned other fairy tales? Or are the newspapers right? Should they be free to operate without public accountability whilst social media platforms are regulated to within an inch of their lives? Should we regulate publishers or platforms? Publishers *and* platforms? *Neither* publishers *nor* platforms?

The old concept of press freedom does not help us solve these puzzles. Like a stuck record, it just spits out the same word, over and over again: *freedom, freedom, freedom...* But trying to think about the modern media using only the concept of 'press freedom' is like using a very old hammer to crack a very modern nut. Either it will miss the nut entirely, or it will smash it into smithereens. We need to take a more forensic approach to the challenges that face us today.

In this book, I ask what press freedom means in the age of digital media. Press freedom was not handed down to us from on high, as some of its fundamentalist advocates seem to believe. It is not something that exists 'out there' in the material world, like wind or water. It is an idea that humans invented, and so – I believe – we can reinvent it. The concept and practice of press freedom developed in response to the communications revolution that swept Europe in the sixteenth and seventeenth centuries. If this concept does not help us address the second communications revolution that is now upon us, then perhaps it is time for us to remake it.

If we dare.

Part I

Part I

Making Press Freedom

I F YOU HAD wanted to buy a book in the Middle Ages, you would not have been able to pop into a bookshop. You would have had to commission a scribe to write out your text by hand. You would have received a beautiful object, but the cost would have been eye-watering – comparable to the price of a luxury car today. In monasteries across Europe, monks had been copying and illustrating manuscripts for a thousand years. The most popular existed in a few copies, but many were unique. The canon of available literature was tiny, and largely confined to religious works.

In 1455, everything changed. Johannes Gutenberg perfected the technology he had been developing in secret for several years, and produced the first printed book in Europe. From that point on, readers could get their hands on texts that were far cheaper than anything produced in a scriptorium. Ideas that had once been confined to the elite began to percolate to hundreds, thousands and eventually millions of readers. People who had once questioned Church doctrine in secret now found that they were part of a network of readers who could share and amplify each other's concerns.

These new forms of religious freedom led swiftly to new forms of religious suppression – most notoriously in the form of the Spanish Inquisition, which sentenced as many as 10,000 people to death.[1] In England, the turbulence saw Catholics killed by a Protestant regime, and then Protestants killed by a Catholic regime. Towards the end of the sixteenth century, so-called pamphlet wars broke out, as polemicists on both sides of the argument fought for ideological supremacy.[2]

By the middle of the seventeenth century, there were hundreds of presses at work in London, churning out an incessant supply of books, pamphlets and broadsheets.

---

1   Joseph Pérez, *The Spanish Inquisition: A History*, trans. Janet Lloyd (London: Profile Books, 2004), p. 173.
2   See Cyndia Susan Clegg, *Press Censorship in Elizabethan England* (Cambridge: Cambridge University Press, 1997).

Some of these publications claimed to present the 'news', but they were not newspapers as we know them today. They were more like blogs – first-person accounts of current events, heavily skewed by the political opinions of the author and printer, and calculated to whip up powerful emotions among their readers.

As the tensions between radicals and conservatives gave way to open warfare in the middle of the seventeenth century, people began to ask what to do about this rowdy press. Parliament's first act on seizing power at the outbreak of the Civil War was to abolish the Star Chamber – the royal court that had controlled the printing industry. But then, faced with a tidal wave of unlicensed publications, parliamentarians – most of whom were middle-class, property-owning men – thought again, and reintroduced censorship. It was now that the concept of press freedom began to take shape.

Truth

John Milton is best known today as the author of *Paradise Lost*, the epic poem which sets out to justify the ways of God to men. But to his contemporaries, he was a pamphleteer who intervened noisily in the political debates of his day. In response to the Licensing Order of 1643, Milton published a short but passionate pamphlet, *Areopagitica*. 'Who ever knew truth put to the worse in a free and open encounter?' he demanded to know.[3]

Areopagitica is the first extended argument for press freedom. In it, Milton argued that even well-intentioned censorship might have terrible consequences: the state would become too powerful, debate would be stifled and the truth would be obscured.

When we talk about press freedom now, we are invoking Milton as our guide, whether we know it or not. And so it is important to understand what he meant. Otherwise, we might get tangled up in ideas that have long passed their sell-by date.

Milton addressed himself to 'the true wayfaring Christian' who 'can apprehend and consider vice with all her baits and seeming pleasures, and yet abstain, and

3 *Areopagitica*, in John Milton, *The Major Works*, ed. Stephen Orgel and Jonathan Goldberg (Oxford: Oxford University Press, 2003), pp. 236–73.

yet distinguish, and yet prefer that which is truly better'. Like the hero of *The Pilgrim's Progress*, by Milton's
contemporary John Bunyan, this imaginary Christian
is committed to the discovery of truth. Milton advised
such wayfarers to read 'any books whatever come to
thy hands, for thou art sufficient both to judge right,
and to examine each matter'. He argued that even if
'all the winds of doctrine were let loose to play upon
the earth', so long as the truth is out there, 'we do inju-
riously by licensing and prohibiting … misdoubt her
strength'. Milton concluded, 'Let her and falsehood
grapple; who ever knew truth put to the worse in a free
and open encounter. Her confuting is the best and surest
suppressing.'

In other words, the state should not suppress publications simply because they consist of lies. We should
allow the public to decide what is true and what is
false. Just as free market economists believe that mar-
kets will always set the right value on all goods and
services, so Milton believed that 'free and open' debate
would always set the right value on truth. His image of

truth and falsehood clashing with each other came to be known as 'the marketplace of ideas'. It is one of the three pillars of press freedom.

Imagine that you walk into a crowded market. From every side, you are assailed by hawkers and hustlers. A conspiracy theory here! A piece of malicious gossip over there! A distortion of the facts at cut price! You wander from stall to stall, overwhelmed by claim and counterclaim, until eventually you find a trader who calmly and clearly sets out the facts of the matter. *It's over here!* you shout over your shoulder, and everyone streams after you to the vendor of truth, overturning the tables of falsehood on their way.

This is more or less what Milton had in mind. His vision was not shared by the parliament of his day, but it has given succour to newspaper publishers ever since. They have seized on the marketplace metaphor to argue that there should be no restrictions on their freedom – because even if they sometimes get things wrong, the truth will always prevail. *Areopagitica* has been quoted in this way in free speech cases in the English and American courts. Even Rupert Murdoch's News International cited Milton in its opening submission to the Leveson Inquiry – a bold move for a company that was implicated in wide-ranging allegations of deceit.[4]

As the Leveson Inquiry progressed, I revisited Milton's landmark essay. I wanted to find out whether Milton would have supported Murdoch's arguments against regulation. Did Milton really believe in an absolute form of press freedom? The more of *Areopagitica* I read, the more puzzled I became. I had no trouble finding the resounding phrases that are often quoted in support of press freedom. But I found other things as well: aspects of Milton's argument that have been ignored or forgotten by press freedom fundamentalists like Brendan O'Neill, who deplores 'the policing of thought' in Britain – 'this nation that gave the world John Milton and his *Areopagitica*'.[5]

For a start, Milton did not object in the least to 'the policing of thought'. In fact, he was strongly in favour

---

4   See https://discoverleveson.com/evidence/Opening_Submission_on_behalf_of_News_International/9541/media.

5   Brendan O'Neill, 'Britain Turns Offensive Speech into a Police Matter', *Reason*, 15 September 2018, available at https://reason.com/2018/09/15/britain-turns-offensive-speech-into-a-po/.

of criminal laws such as blasphemy and sedition, which allow the state to punish the publication of material that disrupts the status quo. Furthermore, Milton was not defending the rights of the news media. When he wrote about 'the press', he did not mean newspapers in the modern sense – there were none in 1644. He was defending pamphlets like his own, alongside works of poetry, history and theology. He had never heard of *The Sun*.

Thirdly, Milton was not arguing against all forms of regulation. When he wrote about the freedom of the press, he meant the freedom from censorship – where a state official reviews books before they are published – not a general freedom from law or regulation. He was in favour of some form of licensing, saying that no book should be printed 'unless the printer's and the author's name, or at least the printer's be registered'. And he even called for the death sentence to be imposed on publishers who printed books that were 'mischievous and libellous' – material for which 'the fire and the executioner will be the timeliest and the most effectual remedy'.

Finally – and perhaps most significantly – Milton was coming at the question of censorship from a religious perspective. He was not proposing a relativist's account of the truth, in which all truths are equal, or a scientist's account, in which all truths can be tested and objectively demonstrated, but a *Protestant*'s truth, in which revelation comes to those who have the right kind of faith:

> Truth indeed came once into the world with her divine Master, and was a perfect shape most glorious to look on: but when he ascended, and his Apostles after him were laid asleep, then straight arose a wicked race of deceivers, who [...] took the Virgin Truth, hewed her lovely form into a thousand pieces, and scattered them to the four winds.

In other words, the truth of Christianity was present in Christ but corrupted by the Catholic Church. Milton was arguing that his readers – as good 'wayfaring' Protestants – should aim to rediscover this truth, through learning, debate and argument, if necessary – but not by questioning the essence of faith itself.

In short, Milton's pamphlet was an argument not for an absolute form of press freedom but for a limited form of religious freedom. Milton thought that authors and publishers should be free to pursue the truth about their Christian faith – subject to statutory regulation. He thought that publishers should be free from censorship – but bound by strict laws of libel, sedition and blasphemy. He thought that publishers should be free to print what they liked without prior restraint – but executed if they broke the law. When he talked about 'the truth', he was referring to the kind of personal or religious truth that we would now call 'faith', or 'opinion'. He was certainly not saying that publishers should be free to publish false facts. This is hardly a resounding defence of the rights of newspapers to publish lies and distortions.

In any case, the whole premise of the marketplace of ideas is pretty shaky. Anyone who is seriously interested in the truth about objective reality (rather than religious faith or opinion) would not leave it to the market to discover. That is not how we conduct science or law, for example. Scientists are not free to say what they *think* is true: they must provide evidence to demonstrate their findings. Likewise, lawyers might argue vigorously against each other in court, but their primary duty is to the principle of justice. They are not allowed to lie. Lawyers can be struck off for breaking the rules, and scientists can lose their jobs if they fabricate evidence.

As the philosopher Onora O'Neill has observed, 'truth-seeking needs careful process and safeguards; freedom to propose and challenge content, for example, but not freedom to neglect or travesty evidence'.[6] Bernard Williams wrote that

> in institutions that are expressly dedicated to finding out the truth, such as universities, research institutes, and courts of law, speech is not at all unregulated. People cannot come in from outside, speak when they feel like it, make endless irrelevant, or insulting, interventions, and so on; they cannot invoke a right to do so, and no one thinks that things would go better in the direction of truth if they could.[7]

---

6 Onora O'Neill, 'Conceptions of Press Freedom in a Globalising World' (2008), available at https://www.repository.cam.ac.uk/bitstream/handle/1810/241043/Press_freedom_oneill_2008.pdf;sequence=1.

7 Bernard Williams, *Truth and Truthfulness: An Essay in Genealogy* (Princeton, NJ: Princeton University Press, 2002), p. 217.

Scientists and lawyers are free to go about their business without state interference. In fact, they would fight fiercely against any political meddling. Nonetheless, they accept a high degree of regulation, in order to protect the integrity of their professions.

We do not expect the truth to emerge in science or law through some kind of mysterious encounter with falsehood. So why on earth do we think that this will happen in the news media? To answer that question, we need to fast-forward almost 200 years, from the religious turbulence of the mid-seventeenth century to the political turbulence of the mid-nineteenth century, just as modern journalism was starting to take shape.

Democracy

Charles Dickens joined the reporters in the gallery of the House of Commons in 1831. It was his first writing job, and although his parliamentary journalism lacks the punch of his novels and short stories (he basically just transcribed politicians' speeches for publication), his presence in the gallery gives us a window into a forgotten world.

Since its earliest days in the thirteenth century, the English Parliament had been closed to outsiders. What happened in Parliament stayed in Parliament, and to write about it was a crime. In 1763, John Wilkes was convicted of seditious libel after reporting on a parliamentary speech. When Wilkes overturned his conviction, Parliament began to open up to public view. Thomas Hansard started printing records of parliamentary debates in 1809, and his name is still used for the transcripts of each day's proceedings that are published today. He was followed by Dickens's uncle, John Henry Barrow, who gave the ambitious nineteen-year-old a job on his fledgling newspaper, the *Mirror of Parliament*.

Dickens later recalled looking down into the Commons from the gallery:

> The body of the House and the side galleries are full of Members; some, with their legs on the back of the opposite seat; some, with theirs stretched out to their utmost length on the floor; some going out, others coming in; all talking, laughing, lounging, coughing, oh-ing, questioning, or groaning; presenting a conglomeration of

noise and confusion, to be met with in no other place
in existence, not even excepting Smithfield on a market
day, or a cockpit in its glory.[8]

Thomas Macaulay, writing in 1828, described the parliamentary reporters up in the gallery as the 'fourth estate' of the realm – an appellation that has stuck ever since. The first three 'estates' were made up of the bishops, peers and MPs who sat in the Houses of Parliament. By describing the press as a fourth estate, Macaulay was giving journalists equal status with lawmakers, and setting in train an idea that has gained momentum ever since – that the press has an elevated position, above and beyond democracy, acting as a check and balance on politicians, but not condescending to join them in the bear pit below.

This notion of the fourth estate stands alongside the image of the marketplace of ideas as the second pillar of the press freedom myth. It is deployed by press freedom advocates to argue that the news media must not

8   *Dickens' Journalism: Sketches by Boz and Other Early Papers 1833–39*, ed. Michael Slater (London: J. M. Dent, 1994), p. 156.

be regulated by the state, because it is the job of journalists to hold the state to account.

However, the relationship between the media and the state is much more complicated than this label suggests. Up in the gallery, Dickens may have been physically removed from the fray, but he was deeply affected by the emotions of what went on below. When the Irish MP Daniel O'Connell described the sufferings of the Irish poor, Dickens reportedly 'put down his pencil … and declared he could not take notes of the speech, so moved was he by its pathos'.[9] And he was hardly an impartial witness of events, describing Tories as 'people whom, politically, I despise and abhor'.[10]

Journalists are human beings. They have a stake in the political action, just as politicians have a stake in the media. Politicians want to get their message across. They want to earn a living. They want to build support for their policies – or to find policies that come

9 See Robert Douglas-Fairhurst, *Becoming Dickens: The Invention of a Novelist* (Cambridge, MA: Harvard University Press, 2011), p. 79.
10 *The Pilgrim Edition of the Letters of Charles Dickens*, Vol. 2, p. 379, cited in Douglas-Fairhurst, ibid., p. 77.

with ready-made support. The press can help with all of these things, but news publishers have also got skin in the political game. They are not disinterested observers of democracy, living on the moon and watching us through a telescope. They walk among us. In Britain, there has always been an intimate relationship between the world of politics and the world of the media. John Wilkes was both a journalist and a Member of Parliament. His parliamentary reporting was not necessarily motivated by a deep sense of commitment to the public interest, but by his personal stake in the debate.

Sometimes, a publisher supports a politician because they share a belief in a particular issue – immigration reform, say, or healthcare privatisation. Sometimes, however, news publishers support politicians because they have a more immediate interest in what those politicians can do for them.

In 1981, Margaret Thatcher's government accepted undertakings from Rupert Murdoch that he would not seek to exercise editorial control over *The Times* – a newspaper which he was then allowed to add to *The Sun* and the *News of the World* in his bulging portfolio of UK media holdings. According to Sir Harold Evans, who was then the editor of *The Times*, Murdoch's promise was broken almost as soon as it was made.[11] But it was too late. The politicians had accepted the press baron's assurances. And in return, they won his support.

In the early 1990s, politicians again bowed down when Murdoch's papers and others campaigned against effective press regulation. A government minister, David Mellor, said that newspaper owners were 'drinking in the last chance saloon' after a series of scandals in which journalists were found to have breached people's privacy. The actor Gordon Kaye was harassed in his hospital ward by reporters, whilst the television presenter Russell Harty was pictured on his deathbed by photographers who kept him under surveillance from the flat opposite. In response to these intrusions, Mellor dangled the threat of statutory regulation over the press. However, his own moral authority was destroyed when *The Sun* (relying on intercepted phone calls, as it happens)

---

11 Harold Evans, 'How Thatcher and Murdoch made their secret deal', *The Guardian*, 28 April 2015.

caught him in bed with an actress, and the momentum towards regulation was lost.

Murdoch's *Sun* was hardly serving as the fourth estate of the realm in its dealings with Mellor. The paper fabricated elements of the story (falsely claiming that Mellor had made love whilst wearing a Chelsea football kit) to exert maximum humiliation. The effect of this reporting was to destroy a politician who had threatened Rupert Murdoch's autonomy, and to scare off others. I have met numerous public figures over the years who have shied away from questions of press regulation for fear of the consequences. Most people have something in their lives that they would rather keep private. Everyone wants to protect their friends and family from harassment. No one enjoys being the subject of public mockery. After the Leveson Inquiry, it emerged that the Murdoch papers held compromising material on public figures and celebrities in a huge safe in *The Sun*'s newsroom.[12] This material was not necessarily intended for publication,

---

12 Martin Hickman, 'Life and death in the Sun newsroom', openDemocracy, 26 October 2015, available at https://www.opendemocracy.net/en/opendemocracyuk/life-and-death-in-sun-newsroom/.

and few people knew exactly what was inside the safe. But, like the invisible eye of Big Brother in Orwell's *Nineteen Eighty-Four*, its mere existence had a powerful effect, allowing Murdoch's papers to hint at the risk of exposure whenever anyone got in their way. Some politicians, cowed by this threat, have called it blackmail.[13]

This is the paradox of the fourth estate. Media companies do not just serve society. They also serve their own commercial and political interests. Newspapers can promote policies by suppressing the alternatives. They can support political parties by suppressing positive news about other parties. They might like a party because they agree with its policies or simply because it has promised to protect their business interests. Either way, they can choose not to investigate the activities of certain politicians whilst making a big noise about what others are getting up to. They are under no obligation to give us the full range of information that we need in order to make democratic decisions. Newspapers argue that they are playing a vital democratic role as

13 See Tom Watson MP's evidence to the Leveson Inquiry, available at https://discoverleveson.com/hearing/2012-05-22/998/?bc=3.

the fourth estate, but they do not guarantee the scrutiny and investigative functions that we need for a healthy democracy. In fact, an absolutely 'free' press is always at risk of being captured by an unholy alliance of political and corporate forces.

In the United States, President Donald Trump has long enjoyed a cosy relationship with two big media companies, American Media, Inc. (AMI) and Fox News. In December 2018, AMI, which publishes the *National Enquirer*, told prosecutors that it had 'worked "in concert" with Trump's campaign when it bought Karen McDougal's story of a sexual affair with Trump, which it suppressed "to prevent it from influencing the election"'.[14] Trump's friendship with Fox News and its chairman, Rupert Murdoch, is so intimate that Fox has been described as 'the closest we've come to having state TV' in the US.[15]

I have seen what happens when politicians control

---

14 Jon Swaine, 'National Enquirer owner admits to "catch and kill" payment to ex-playmate', *The Guardian*, 12 December 2018.

15 Jane Mayer, 'The Making of the Fox News White House', *New Yorker*, 4 March 2019.

the media, in countries from Azerbaijan to Zimbabwe, and I firmly believe that the press should not be under the thumb of the state. But I have also seen what happens when the state is under the thumb of the press. Freedom, in this case, can mean freedom from accountability – for both press barons *and* politicians – as much as freedom from state control.

Self-expression

According to the marketplace of ideas theory, it is better to endure lies than to regulate the press, because people are able to sift out truths from falsehoods. According to the fourth estate theory, the press should be free from oversight because reporters play a unique role in democracy. Taken together (as they always are by press freedom advocates), these two notions assert that the press must be free from regulation so that it can serve the causes of truth and democracy. The third pillar of press freedom is the theory of self-expression, developed by the nineteenth-century philosopher John Stuart Mill.

Mill strained against the social norms of his day. He

had a long relationship with a woman who was married to another man. He advocated the rights of women to vote. But in other respects, he was a figure of his times, who thought that British imperialism was necessary to bring civilisation to inferior cultures. Nonetheless, he set out to break the moral chains that limited people's freedom in Victorian Britain.

In his ground-breaking essay *On Liberty*, Mill argued that (white, European) people should be entirely free, so long as they did not limit the freedom of others.[16] He believed that, in order to flourish as human beings, we should enjoy freedom – not only freedom of thought ('liberty of conscience, in the most comprehensive sense'), but also freedom of expression and freedom of association. Mill thought that, by allowing people to realise their potential, freedom would benefit both the individual and society as a whole: 'In proportion to the development of his individuality, each person becomes more valuable to himself, and is, therefore, capable of being more valuable to others.'

16 John Stuart Mill, *On Liberty and Other Essays*, ed. John Gray (Oxford: Oxford University Press, 1991).

However, Mill could see that there are times when our pursuit of self-expression crashes into the freedom of others. We cannot be free to kill each other or lock each other up just because we feel like it. He said that freedom should have limits. We should therefore only enjoy the freedom 'of pursuing our own good in our own way, *so long as we do not attempt to deprive others of theirs, or impede their efforts to obtain it*'.[17] To resolve the conflicts between different people's freedoms, Mill set out 'one very simple principle' which he believed should govern the relationship between society and the individual: 'That the only purpose for which power can be rightfully exercised over any member of a civilized community, against his will, is to prevent harm to others.' In other words, governments may pass laws, and communities may impose moral norms, if – *and only if* – this is necessary to stop people from harming each other, not just because the people at the top of society want to control everyone else's business.

This was a radical challenge to the social and political structures of the day. Rather than asking people to

---

17 My emphasis.

defend their wish to be free, Mill asked the state to justify its attempts to limit their freedom. Mill's so-called harm principle pumped the oxygen of liberty into the stifling moral conventions of the mid-nineteenth century and turned the relationship between the state and the individual on its head. It still helps us to think about freedom today. It suggests that we should all be free to pursue our own good, in our own way – whether that means practising yoga, eating pork, wearing headscarves, getting tattooed, indulging in anal sex or playing the bagpipes – so long as we do not cause harm to others.

Like the vision of the marketplace of ideas and the fourth estate, Mill's harm principle is often cited by press freedom advocates to argue that newspapers – and, in particular, newspaper columnists – should be free to 'express themselves' as Mill envisaged. Tim Luckhurst, a former editor of *The Scotsman*, cited Mill in his evidence to the Leveson Inquiry, describing *On Liberty* as 'a core text for all interested in the purposes journalism serves in representative democracies'.[18] I disagree.

---

18 Available at https://discoverleveson.com/evidence/Submission_by_Professor_
Tim_Luckhurst/11497/media.

On Liberty may help us think about freedom in general, but it does not have much to tell us about press freedom in particular.

Media companies are not individuals. Journalists are performing a social function, not pursuing the 'fullness of life' that Mill envisaged. They are seeking not to pursue their own good in their own way, but to inform the public on matters of general interest, and they are employed by companies whose only legal form of 'fullness' is financial, not psychological. In order to provide useful information, journalists are bound by certain moral expectations – for example, that they should try to get their facts straight. These expectations have been codified in journalism rulebooks since the start of the twentieth century. The rules of journalism vary between countries and cultures, but they share some common features, of which fact-checking is the most fundamental.[19]

You and I are not generally obliged to tell the truth.

---

19 See 'IMPRESS Standards Code: Consultation Response Paper' (2017), available at https://impress.press/downloads/file/code/impress-code-consultation-response.pdf, for a recent analysis of the core standards of journalism, as set out in fifty-six standards codes from around the world.

Most of the time, we are quite free to lie to each other, to our friends and colleagues and even to the world at large. We can repeat rumours and hearsay. We can 'pursue our own good, in our own way', by making things up, if that is what turns us on. It is different for journalists. When journalists stand up in public – or in the pages of a newspaper – they implicitly say two things: firstly, *this is the truth*; and secondly, *I can guarantee that this is the truth because I am a journalist*. This guarantee is underwritten by the rules of journalism, whereby journalists are expected to check their facts and verify their sources.

In recognition of the valuable role they play, newspaper publishers in the UK enjoy a range of legal and commercial privileges. Printed newspapers are zero-rated for value-added tax (VAT), and local authorities are obliged to advertise in local newspapers. Together, these measures have been estimated to amount to an effective subsidy of £250 million per year.[20] Journalists enjoy exemptions

---

20 Lauren Pennycook, 'Why local websites deserve a share of government's £250m-plus annual subsidy for local news', *Press Gazette*, 29 April 2014, available at https://www.pressgazette.co.uk/why-local-websites-deserve-a-share-of-governments-250m-plus-annual-subsidy-for-local-news/.

under the Human Rights Act 1998 and the Data Protection Act 2018. They have an enhanced status under the Defamation Act 2013. Some newspaper editors are privately notified of intelligence issues by the Defence Notice Committee (known as the D-Notice Committee).

Without rules, journalism would be no more than self-expression, and no more – or less – deserving of these privileges than any other kind of speech. With these rules in place, journalism is elevated to a higher status. It plays a socially valuable role, and earns the trust of society. When journalism breaks the rules, it breaks its implicit contract with society and loses its right to be trusted.

The press freedom myth

The marketplace of ideas, the fourth estate and Mill's theory of self-expression have all been used to define and defend the freedom of the press. There are important insights in all of these concepts, but they blind us to the way the media really operates in a modern, democratic society.

The marketplace of ideas suggests that the press must be free in order for the truth to emerge. But when it comes down to the really important decisions in our lives, we do not rely on the marketplace of ideas. We want to know what is true and what is false. Genuinely truth-seeking disciplines, like science and law, benefit from regulation. So does advertising. As consumers, we want to know that things will do what they say on the tin, and we want to know that advertisers will be punished if they lie. We take these forms of regulation for granted. An unregulated marketplace of ideas is an attractive fantasy, but little more.

The notion of the fourth estate says that we should not regulate the press because regulation will inhibit democracy. However, this ignores the way that a free media can short-change democracy, by allowing politicians and media owners to scratch each other's backs in private. A free press may be necessary for democracy, but it is not sufficient. We cannot live without a media that is free from political control, but we cannot live *with* a media that is allowed to subvert the democratic process. Journalists can play a role as the fourth estate, but only if and when they meet certain ethical standards. And how can we be sure that journalists are meeting these standards if they are not regulated?

Political parties in the UK are regulated to ensure that they do not breach spending limits, that their donors are identified, and that they do not make wild claims about their opponents during elections. Television and radio broadcasters in the UK are regulated by an independent statutory body, Ofcom, to uphold impartiality, present both sides in any political debate and ensure that audiences are not misled. Does the democratic sky fall on our heads? No. In fact, broadcasters command higher trust than newspapers, and they are doing better in the face of digital competition than their counterparts in the press.[21] News publishers are exempt from these regulations, although they probably have as much influence on elections as any other player.

The twentieth-century philosopher Isaiah Berlin argued that there are two dimensions of freedom,

---

21 'Reuters Institute Digital News Report 2018', ed. Nic Newman, Richard Fletcher, Antonis Kalogeropoulos, David A. L. Levy and Rasmus Kleis Nielsen (Oxford: Reuters Institute for the Study of Journalism, 2018), p. 42.

negative and positive. He described negative liberty as the *freedom from* something, and positive liberty as the *freedom to* do something. We say that the press must be *free from* political control (negative liberty) *in order to* advance the causes of truth, democracy and self-expression (positive liberty). Newspaper apologists like to blur the distinction between the two halves of this argument. They maintain that simply by being free from political control, the press will provide all the benefits of truth, democracy and self-expression.

However, the relationship between the positive and negative dimensions of press freedom does not work like that. The negative liberty of the press does not lead magically to a world of truth, democracy and self-expression. In fact, an entirely free media, with no obligation to respect the standards of journalism, is just as likely to obscure the truth, subvert democracy and erode individual freedoms. The press freedom myth is part of the truth, but it is not the whole truth about the relationship between the media and society. The reality is far more complex.

Part II

Shaking Press Freedom

OVER THE YEARS, I have met hundreds of foreign journalists. At first, I was surprised when they rolled their eyes at any mention of the British press. Over time, I got used to it. Our tabloids in particular are seen as raucous, divisive and careless with the facts. Even their own readers do not rate them highly. Fewer than 10 per cent of the British population trust tabloids to tell the truth.[22] Our newspapers are in fact the least trusted in Europe, with a lower rating than the press of comparatively fragile states such as North Macedonia, Serbia and Greece.[23]

---

22 Brian Cathcart, 'Trust, newspapers and journalists: a review of evidence', *Radical Statistics*, Vol. 118 (2017), 3–19, p. 5.
23 See the Fragile States Index, published by the Fund for Peace: https://fragile statesindex.org/.

This reputation is not entirely fair. Over the years, British newspapers of all shapes and sizes – both tabloids and broadsheets – have told important stories in the public interest. In May 2009, the *Daily Telegraph* exposed the abuse of the expenses system by Members of the UK Parliament. Between 2011 and 2012, Andrew Norfolk published a series of stories in *The Times* about child sexual exploitation in Rotherham. In 2013, *The Guardian* revealed how British and American spies were routinely eavesdropping on people's private telephone and email communications.

These stories won acclaim for their reporters and editors. At awards ceremonies, they slapped each other on the back, proud to be involved in such important work. But journalists do not always get it right. And maybe it is the mistakes – compounded by that air of self-congratulation – that puts people off the British press.

In 2011, *The Guardian* revealed that reporters from the *News of the World* had hacked into the mobile phone messages of Milly Dowler, a schoolgirl who had disappeared nine years earlier. In the days after her disappearance, Milly's parents and the police had been checking her phone messages on the off-chance that they might learn something about her whereabouts. When old messages began disappearing, they thought that Milly must be picking up the messages as well. 'She's alive!' exclaimed her mother, only to have her hopes crushed when Milly's body was found.[24]

It was alleged that the deletions were the fault of *News of the World* journalists and the private investigators who worked for them. In fact, it is possible that the messages were automatically deleted when the voicemail system reached its capacity. Either way, those journalists took no responsibility for the impact of their actions on Milly or her family. They were looking for a front-page story, not a missing girl.

Public outrage grew when it became clear that the hacking of Milly Dowler's phone was not an isolated incident. Journalists across the industry had been listening in to private phone messages as an easy way of generating stories. Under pressure to get a scoop, they sat at their desks and dialled in to people's voicemail.

---

24 See https://discoverleveson.com/hearing/2011-11-21/927/?bc=7.

They presumably told themselves that what they were doing was in the 'public interest' – because they were journalists, and journalists are the good guys.

But the public – when they found out about it – disagreed. They thought that phone hacking was wrong and that newspapers should be more effectively regulated.[25] In response to mounting pressure, the government asked a senior judge, Sir Brian Leveson, to lead an inquiry into the phone-hacking scandal. Sir Brian was told that he was free to propose new laws and regulations and that the government would act on his recommendations – so long as they were not, in David Cameron's word, 'bonkers'.

My friends in the newspaper industry were concerned from the outset that the Leveson Inquiry would lead to a new and more robust form of press regulation. They had every reason to be worried. Leveson soon unearthed behaviour that went way beyond phone hacking. He revealed that some papers were not merely partisan but so biased that they were going out of their way to find

25   For a summary of public polling on press regulation, see Gordon Neil Ramsay, 'How Newspapers Covered Press Regulation After Leveson' (London: Media Standards Trust, September 2014), pp. 73–95.

stories that suited their prejudices – to stigmatise Muslims, for example, or asylum-seekers. When they could not find a true story, they made one up.[26] Newspaper editors rushed to print false front-page stories, only to hide tiny corrections, months later, as far inside the paper as possible. Some of these stories accused people of serious crimes – rape, murder or child abuse. Sometimes the papers were sued for libel, but the damages they paid out were less than the profits they made from these sensational headlines, and far less important than the power they wielded over public life, thanks to their huge share of the media market. Newspapers that are read by millions can, quite literally, tell governments what to do.

Sir Brian – and the public who watched the inquiry live online – heard about forms of journalism which he would later describe in the most damning terms:

> There have been too many times when, chasing the story, parts of the press have acted as if its own code, which it

---

26 See the evidence provided by Richard Peppiatt to the Leveson Inquiry about his experiences as a young journalist at the *Daily Star*, available at https://discoverleveson.com/hearing/2011-11-29/932/?bc=10.

wrote, simply did not exist. This has caused real hardship and, on occasion, wreaked havoc with the lives of innocent people whose rights and liberties have been disdained. This is not just the famous but ordinary members of the public, caught up in events (many of them, truly tragic) far larger than they could cope with but made much, much worse by press behaviour that, at times, can only be described as outrageous.[27]

For decades, the largest British newspapers had claimed to regulate themselves through the Press Complaints Commission (PCC), a private organisation that was established by – and accountable to – the publishers who paid its bills. As the inquiry progressed, most witnesses from the industry accepted that the PCC had never really been a regulator at all. It had handled individual complaints, but it could not stop publishers from doing what they liked. It had never imposed a fine. It had never demanded a front-page correction. And it had

---

27 Lord Justice Leveson, 'An Inquiry into the Culture, Practices and Ethics of the Press: Executive Summary' (London: The Stationery Office, November 2012), p. 4.

not investigated phone hacking, even after *The Guard-ian* published serious allegations about the extent of the problem. In fact, the PCC had issued a derisory report, saying that *The Guardian*'s allegations were all mouth and no trousers.[28]

As director of English PEN, the free speech charity, I was asked to give evidence to the Leveson Inquiry about the value of a free press. But, sitting in a witness box at the High Court, I struggled to explain why the freedom of the press was more important than other people's freedom to get on with their lives. I argued that, although self-regulation under the PCC had failed, statutory regulation (where the government sets up a regulator by Act of Parliament) would be even worse, as it would allow politicians to control the press. I told Leveson that there was no 'magical way' between the 'rock' of self-regulation and the 'hard place' of statu-tory regulation, and that he might 'ultimately have to choose the rock or the hard place'.[29] Leveson was not

---

28 See Nick Davies, *Hack Attack: How the truth caught up with Rupert Mur-doch* (London: Chatto & Windus, 2014), p. 129.

29 See https://discoverleveson.com/hearing/2012-01-24/953/?bc=13.

particularly impressed by this challenge. 'It's not difficult to remove the scope of politicians,' he observed.

One day, I turned up at the inquiry to see a mid-
dle-aged woman standing alone on the far side of an
empty hallway. She looked lost, daunted by the scale of
the building. It was Sally Dowler, Milly's mother. My
heart went out to her, and, inside, something began to
change. I had what religious believers would call a crisis of faith.

I still believed in the value of journalism and the
importance of press freedom. But I could not understand why powerless people like Sally Dowler should
have to suffer for that freedom. Why should she – and
the thousands of other phone-hacking victims – have to
pay such a heavy price, whilst the billionaire owners of
the press got away scot-free? No one was hacking into
their phones, or writing about *their* private lives. The
publishers of Britain's largest newspapers were wealthy
men: Rupert Murdoch, Richard Desmond, Viscount
Rothermere and Sir David and Sir Frederick Barclay.
Was it right that our freedom should be in their hands?

Leveson concluded that it was not. He accepted that

self-regulation of the press was better than statutory regulation, but he said that the self-regulator should be accountable to a public body to ensure that its procedures were fair and that it did not go native, as the PCC had done. In effect, he was proposing something like an MOT or a company audit. Politicians do not personally tinker with your car or scrutinise your accounts, but they are responsible for the integrity of those regulatory regimes.

I thought that Leveson had found a way between the rock and the hard place. However, the dominant publishers spurned his proposals in favour of their own body, IPSO (the Independent Press Standards Organisation), a rebranded version of the PCC which failed to meet most of Leveson's criteria for independence or effectiveness.

The public watched helplessly as the sign on the door of the PCC was removed and replaced with a sign for IPSO. The same men who had controlled the PCC continued to occupy powerful positions in relation to IPSO. Paul Dacre, then editor of the *Daily Mail*, remained in place as chair of the Editors' Code of Practice Committee, which wrote the rules that IPSO was supposed to enforce. And so, unsurprisingly, many of the issues that had dogged the press before Leveson kept on coming in the years following the inquiry. Meanwhile, the apologists for the newspaper industry continued to rely on the press freedom myth to defend their actions.

Self-expression and the press

In December 2012 – only a month after Leveson had delivered his report – a schoolteacher called Lucy Meadows attracted the attention of the *Daily Mail* columnist Richard Littlejohn. He accused Meadows of projecting her 'personal problems on to impressionable young children' and forcing 'some of the more challenging realities of adult life' down children's throats.[30]

What had Miss Meadows done to outrage Littlejohn? She had committed the cardinal sin of changing her sex. Up until the end of the autumn term, Lucy Meadows had been known as Nathan Upton. Just before the Christmas

---

30 See Roy Greenslade, 'Daily Mail urged to fire Richard Littlejohn after death of Lucy Meadows', *The Guardian*, 22 March 2013.

holidays, the school sent out a letter to parents with a short paragraph about Mr Upton, who – parents were told – 'has recently made a significant change in his life and will be transitioning to live as a woman. After the Christmas break, she will return to work as Miss Meadows.'[31]

Some parents were supportive of the new Miss Meadows. Others were unsettled. One contacted the media. Lucy's ex-wife has described what happened next: 'The first and most visible consequence of "press interest" is the press pack turning up on your doorstep. They appeared, en masse, to besiege Lucy in her home. Reporters. Photographers. Camera crew. You name it.'[32]

Three months later, Lucy was dead. In her suicide note, she did not blame the press, but at her inquest, the coroner accused the *Daily Mail* of 'ridicule', 'humilia-tion' and 'character assassination'. In closing, he turned to the reporters present and said, 'And to you the press, I say shame, shame on all of you.'[33]

---

31 See Ruth Smith, 'Lucy Meadows was a transgender teacher who took her own life. Her story must be remembered', *The Independent*, 19 November 2017.

32 Ibid.

33 Helen Pidd, 'Lucy Meadows coroner tells press: "shame on you"', *The Guardian*, 28 May 2013.

It should go without saying that Richard Littlejohn did not kill Lucy Meadows. It is not clear whether his column led to her suicide. However, it is blindingly obvious that it did not help. He compounded the pressure on a vulnerable young woman at a crucial point in her life. He encouraged others to view her decision as selfish, or even aggressive towards the children in her care. And he gave moral cover to the paparazzi and others who descended upon Lucy and her family at a time when they desperately needed some privacy.

Littlejohn, and other representatives of the press, behaved as though Lucy's life were simply an object for media consumption. And why, in their view, was the story of Miss Meadows so newsworthy? It was not as though they wanted to reward her for pursuing her own good in her own way. No. They wanted to blame her for daring to be different.

In his column, Littlejohn claimed that he did not oppose Lucy's transition: he just thought she should have got a job in a different school, where the children had not known her as Mr Upton. But this only makes sense if you agree with Littlejohn that a trans person should not be free to express their identity at the same time as holding down the job they love. The logical conclusion of Littlejohn's argument is that Lucy should not have undergone sex reassignment surgery *and* kept her job. She should, in other words, have been forced to choose between one fundamentally important aspect of her identity and another. That is a choice that, in a free society, none of us should be forced to make.

For the most part, the gatekeepers of the old media have brought a prurient morality to bear on other people's lives whilst keeping their own lifestyles under wraps. After the phone-hacking scandal, it emerged that the editors of *The Sun* and the *News of the World*, Rebekah Brooks and Andy Coulson, had been having an affair at the same time as sending out reporters and photographers to expose other people's indiscretions. They justified their scoops on the grounds of the 'public interest', but saw no similar public interest in their own carryings-on.

Whenever they are accused of overstepping the mark, newspaper columnists invoke their right to express themselves. *It's not like we're doing any harm, are we?*

It's only words! What is this – the Spanish Inquisition?
No matter that these outrage merchants are themselves,
more often than not, seeking to impose their strait-laced
morality on the freedoms of others: gay people, trans
people, single mothers, benefit-claimants, Muslims.
They are 'only expressing themselves'. And who are
we to gainsay them?

Thus, in order to 'express' herself, Katie Hopkins can
write in *The Sun* that migrants are like 'cockroaches'
and that some British towns are 'festering sores' where
the authorities are 'shelling out benefits like Monopoly
money'.[34] In order to 'express' himself, Kelvin Mac-
Kenzie can write (also in *The Sun*) that a young woman
should not have been allowed to present the television
news on the night of a terror attack – because, like the
perpetrators of the attack, she was a Muslim.[35] In order
to 'express' himself, Trevor Kavanagh can highlight (also,
as it happens, in *The Sun*) sexual offences committed by

---

34 Katie Hopkins, 'Rescue boats? I'd use gunships to stop migrants', *The Sun*,
17 April 2015.

35 Kelvin MacKenzie, 'Why did Channel 4 have a presenter in a hijab fronting
coverage of Muslim terror in Nice?', *The Sun*, 18 July 2016.

Muslim men, and ask his readers what 'we' are going to do about 'The Muslim Problem'.[36]

These three writers used their columns to argue that asylum-seekers and Muslims should not be treated with the same dignity as other citizens. In exercising their freedom, they attempted to deprive others of theirs. Yet IPSO rejected complaints against all three, on the grounds that they were simply expressing their opinions – as though their columns constituted nothing more serious than games with words.

In the case of Katie Hopkins, IPSO ruled that she 'was entitled to present her view that the level of support paid to asylum seekers by the British government was too high'.[37] Likewise, IPSO endorsed Kelvin MacKenzie's freedom 'to engage in discussion, criticism and debate about religious ideas and practices, including the wearing of religious symbols while reading the news'.[38]

---

36 Trevor Kavanagh, 'Now Phil's finally Out, he must shut door behind him', *The Sun*, 14 August 2017.

37 Available at https://www.ipso.co.uk/rulings-and-resolution-statements/ruling/?id=02741-15.

38 Available at https://www.ipso.co.uk/rulings-and-resolution-statements/ruling/?id=05935-16.

IPSO conceded that Kavanagh's reference to 'The Muslim Problem' was capable of causing serious offence – 'given it could be interpreted as a reference to the rhetoric preceding the Holocaust' – but ultimately saw his attack on an entire religious group as no more than a 'comment' on 'the causes of a complex social phenomenon'.[39]

In all three decisions, IPSO found a way to excuse these columnists on the grounds that they were exercising their freedom of expression – as though Hopkins, MacKenzie and Kavanagh were simply enjoying a spot of finger painting or interpretive dance. IPSO seemed oblivious to the irony that, in exercising their freedom, the columnists – and their publisher, Rupert Murdoch – were calling for others to be treated as second-class citizens. IPSO seemed not to understand that it is quite possible to discuss migration policy without dehumanising migrants, to discuss religion without suggesting that every Muslim woman is a terrorist sympathiser, and to discuss sexual offences committed by Muslim men without suggesting that every Muslim is a 'problem'

---

39 Available at https://www.ipso.co.uk/rulings-and-resolution-statements/ruling/?id=17562-17.

for others to solve, as the Nazis 'solved' the 'problem' of European Jews.

We might tolerate these columnists' choice of words if they were necessary for their own self-expression – if they simply could not lead fulfilling lives unless they were free to describe asylum-seekers as 'cockroaches' or Muslims as a 'problem'. But they could easily make these points without whipping up hatred against vulnerable people. They could ask whether it is appropriate for newsreaders to wear religious symbols without calling for a particular newsreader to be removed from the airwaves. They could ask whether there is a relationship between Muslim culture and sexual abuse without saying that every Muslim is a problem to be solved.

This is not just about offensiveness. It is impossible to protect people from feeling offended. Someone might be offended by someone else's politics or sexual preferences or their taste for playing the ukulele. You cannot stop someone expressing themselves simply because someone, somewhere, might take umbrage. That would give too much power to the armchair censors and social media warriors who delight in rattling off complaints about television programmes, artworks and newspaper columns they have not even seen.

No. Hopkins, MacKenzie and Kavanagh were not simply expressing their views. They were trying to encourage others to share their hatred of asylum-seekers and Muslims, not because of anything that asylum-seekers and Muslims have done individually but because – in the eyes of these columnists – *these whole groups* are contemptible. Their columns cross an important line in our culture. On one side of the line is offensive but harmless commentary – insults, jokes, satire and criticism. On the other side of the line is incitement to hatred – commonly known as hate speech.

The Council of Europe defines hate speech as 'all forms of expression which spread, incite, promote or justify racial hatred, xenophobia, anti-Semitism or other forms of hatred based on intolerance, including: intolerance expressed by aggressive nationalism and ethnocentrism, discrimination and hostility against minorities, migrants and people of immigrant origin'.[40] The United Nations

---

40 Available at https://www.coe.int/en/web/freedom-expression/freedom-of-
    expression-and-information-explanatory-memo.

Committee on the Elimination of Racial Discrimination defines hate speech as 'a form of other-directed speech which rejects the core human rights principles of human dignity and equality and seeks to degrade the standing of individuals and groups in the estimation of society'.[41]

The philosopher Jeremy Waldron has argued that hate speech sends two messages to two audiences at the same time. It tells the targeted group that they are not wanted here. And it tells other haters that they are not alone: 'There are enough of us around to make sure these people are not welcome.'[42]

That is what distinguishes hate speech from self-expression of the kind that John Stuart Mill sought to protect. Lucy Meadows should have been free to live her life as a woman. Her decision to do so might offend others, but it did not deprive them of their freedom or cause them any other kind of harm. Littlejohn's column, by contrast, sought to deprive Meadows and other trans people of their freedoms, whilst Hopkins sought to deprive

---

41 Available at https://www.refworld.org/docid/53f457db4.html.

42 Jeremy Waldron, *The Harm in Hate Speech* (Cambridge, MA: Harvard University Press, 2012), p. 2.

asylum-seekers of their rights, and Kavanagh set out to deprive British Muslims of theirs. These columnists were not simply expressing what was in their hearts. Their comments were 'other-directed', or 'other-regarding', as philosophers put it. They were trying to encourage other people to take action. At the very least, they acted hypocritically, in defending their freedom whilst seeking to deprive others of theirs. At worst, they caused real harm.

Recent research has shown that repeated exposure to hate speech can increase prejudice, by normalising the expression of extreme views and desensitising listeners to the shared humanity of the target group.[43] Incendiary language of the kind used by these outrage merchants (references to 'cockroaches' and 'festering sores') activates the amygdala, the most primitive part of the human brain, which responds to perceived threats.[44] This causes the emotions to flare up in a 'fight or flight' response

---

43 See Richard A. Friedman, 'The Neuroscience of Hate Speech', *New York Times*, 31 October 2018.

44 N. Isenberg, D. Silbersweig, A. Engelien, S. Emmerich, K. Malavade, B. Beattie, A. C. Leon and E. Stern, 'Linguistic threat activates the human amygdala', *Proceedings of the National Academy of Sciences of the United States of America*, Vol. 96, No. 18 (1999), 10456–10459.

that cannot easily be overridden by the reasoning parts of the brain. Psychologists have concluded that 'people will nurture and act on their prejudices in the worst ways when these people are put under stress, pressured by peers, or receive approval from authority figures to do so'.[45] Authority figures like high-profile columnists at newspapers that are taken seriously by politicians and broadcasters.[46]

Hatred also has an impact on the groups who are hated, as they internalise the hostility of people around them. Trans and bisexual people, for example, have been found to suffer worse health outcomes than the general population, to an extent that appears to correlate with the amount of discrimination they suffer.[47] Young LGBT people are far more likely than their peers to attempt suicide.[48] When steps are taken to address the

---

45 Susan T. Fiske, 'Look Twice', *Greater Good Magazine*, 1 June 2008, available at https://greatergood.berkeley.edu/article/item/look_twice.

46 The front page of *The Sun* is reviewed every day alongside other newspapers on a range of BBC news programmes, for example.

47 Charles A. Emlet, 'Social, Economic, and Health Disparities Among LGBT Older Adults', *Generations*, Vol. 40, No. 2 (2016), 16–22.

48 See https://www.cdc.gov/lgbthealth/youth.htm.

source of discrimination against these groups, their lives improve.[49]

Words have power, for good and evil. If they did not, we would not have invented language. And we would certainly not have invented the press. Newspapers are intended to be read, and their contents are expected to be acted upon. Newspapers can make or break politicians. They can bring down companies and create heroes out of ordinary people. By the same token, they can spread hatred and promote discrimination.

Mill said that we should enjoy the freedom 'of pursuing our own good in our own way, so long as we do not attempt to deprive others of theirs, or impede their efforts to obtain it'. Littlejohn, Hopkins, Mac-Kenzie and Kavanagh flagrantly broke this rule – whilst implicitly drawing on Mill's philosophy to defend their own actions. They adopted inflammatory language, not because it helps anyone on the path towards self-realisation, but because it generates a powerful

49 See Dhruv Khullar, 'Stigma Against Gay People Can Be Deadly', *New York Times*, 9 October 2018.

emotional response. And emotions are what motivate us to take actions. Such as, for example, buying a newspaper.

Truth and the press

The owners of the *Telegraph* might have been enthusiastic about exposing the corruption of the MPs' expenses system, but they were comparatively coy about holding the banking giant HSBC to account. In 2015, three years after the Leveson Inquiry, the venerable journalist Peter Oborne resigned as the *Telegraph*'s chief political commentator when he discovered that his bosses had been downplaying allegations of tax evasion involving HSBC. It just so happened that HSBC was one of the *Telegraph*'s biggest advertisers.

Oborne claimed that the *Telegraph* had neutralised many other stories to suit its advertisers. 'It is not only the *Telegraph* that is at fault here,' he said. 'The past few years have seen the rise of shadowy executives who determine what truths can and what truths can't be conveyed across the mainstream media.'[50] In effect, he was saying, the *Telegraph*'s version of the truth was being dictated by commercial rather than editorial considerations. When his allegations were picked up by *The Guardian* and the BBC, the *Telegraph* published a pugnacious leader column, asserting that it had 'no regard for the opinions of rival media organisations. None is the paragon of moral or journalistic virtue that their criticisms […] might suggest. All have their own self-serving agendas, both political and commercial.'[51]

Andrew Norfolk was named Journalist of the Year in 2014 for his work on the Rotherham sexual exploitation scandal. Three years later, on 28 August 2017, he published another story about a British child suffering at the hands of Muslims and politically correct social workers. This story concerned a young girl who was placed with Muslim foster carers and made to disown her Christian roots. 'Christian child forced into Muslim foster care', proclaimed the front-page headline in *The*

---

50 Peter Oborne, 'Why I have resigned from the Telegraph', openDemocracy, 17 February 2015, available at https://www.opendemocracy.net/en/opendemocracyuk/why-i-have-resigned-from-telegraph/.

51 'The Telegraph's promise to our readers', *Daily Telegraph*, 19 February 2015.

Times. Unfortunately, the story turned out to be a tissue of errors – not least in that the girl in question had a Muslim background. The whole story unravelled in February 2018, when a judge stated that the press coverage of the case had been detrimental to the interests of the child, who had to be moved from her foster placement under police supervision 'because of the numbers of press in attendance at the foster carer's address'.[52]

Mazher Mahmood boasted to the Leveson Inquiry that his work had led to more than 250 convictions.[53] This figure was probably a wild exaggeration, but the so-called fake sheikh, who operated undercover in the guise of a wealthy Arab, undoubtedly brought down a lot of people over the course of his career. However, it was Mahmood's own wrongdoing that ultimately landed him in jail. A criminal trial found that he had pressured a witness to suppress evidence which showed that – far from being an enthusiastic drug dealer – Tulisa Contostavlos

---

52 A summary of the judgment is available at http://www.transparencyproject.org.uk/press/wp-content/uploads/summary-of-the-judgment-of-her-honour-judge-sapnara-on-16th-february-2018.pdf.

53 See https://discoverleveson.com/hearing/2011-12-12/938/?bc=3.

was in fact fiercely opposed to the use of Class-A drugs. The Crown Prosecution Service subsequently launched a review of twenty-five convictions that had been obtained on the back of Mahmood's sting operations.[54]

The *Telegraph* was right about one thing: newspapers are not paragons of virtue. Nor are they disinterested truth machines. They are companies, owned, run and staffed by human beings with a mixture of motivations. 'All have their own self-serving agendas, both political and commercial.' Newspapers can choose what to investigate and how to investigate it. They might choose to publish the whole truth, a partial truth, or none of the truth. They might create 'truths' of their own, trapping people into doing things they would not otherwise have done. Or they might simply publish falsehoods.

Democracy and the press

To say that some media companies are responsible for spreading lies is not the same as saying that all journalists

---

54   Josh Halliday and Roy Greenslade, 'Fake sheikh Mazher Mahmood cases to be reviewed by CPS', *The Guardian*, 4 December 2014.

are liars. To criticise aspects of the media business is not the same as criticising journalism. Even the most self-serving media company can employ courageous, truth-seeking journalists, such as Marie Colvin, the *Sunday Times* war correspondent who was killed whilst reporting from Syria in 2012. In fact, most journalists go into journalism because they believe in it as a vocation that is as important as it is exciting. They are not likely to make much money out of journalism, which is a precarious way of life at the best of times. They simply want to serve the public interest by discovering stories that are both truthful and socially valuable.

However, the vocational side of journalism is always potentially at odds with the business model of the media. Journalism is a truth-seeking profession that is mostly paid for by advertising, or by proprietors who use their media holdings to promote their political and commercial interests. It is hardly surprising that the truth-telling function of journalism and the self-serving aspects of the media business sometimes rub painfully against each other. The American media scholar Victor Pickard has described these tensions as 'journalism's structural vulnerabilities'.[55] Another American commentator, Jim Sleeper, has observed that the 'conglomerate-driven bottom lining' of the media industry 'short-circuits the arts and disciplines of democratic deliberation'.[56]

Journalism's duty to the public comes under greatest pressure from the interests of the media industry when issues of press regulation are at stake. In the years following the Leveson Inquiry, national newspapers in the UK fell over themselves in their eagerness to tarnish Sir Brian Leveson, his proposals for independent self-regulation, and anyone who dared to support those proposals. Instead of hosting a balanced debate, the dominant players in the press relentlessly promoted their own agenda, as though any form of regulation was unthinkable – even though the only representative voice of British journalists, the National Union

---

55 Victor Pickard, *America's Battle for Media Democracy: The Triumph of Corporate Libertarianism and the Future of Media Reform* (New York, NY: Cambridge University Press, 2015), p. 128.

56 Jim Sleeper, 'The News Media, the Public Sphere and the Phantom Public' (2010), available at http://www.jimsleeper.com/wp-content/uploads/2010/03/the-news-media.pdf.

of Journalists (NUJ), actively *supported* the Leveson recommendations.[57]

David Cameron had vowed to accept whatever recommendations Sir Brian Leveson made. However, he rowed back on this promise as soon as the Leveson Report was published in November 2012. By the spring of 2013, Leveson's recommended statute had been watered down into a royal charter. By the autumn, that charter had been rejected by the press. Three years later, the other elements of Leveson's reforms had still not been introduced, and the promised second part of his inquiry (into criminality within the press and collusion with the police) had been put on hold. Meanwhile, parts of the press continued to publish lies and distortions, and to hack away at the rights of vulnerable people – all in the name of freedom.

In 2016, the government consulted on the completion of the Leveson process, at which point the readers

---

57 See, for example, https://www.nuj.org.uk/campaigns/leveson-inquiry/; https://www.nuj.org.uk/news/nuj-gives-guarded-welcome-to-new-regulatory-framework/; and https://www.nuj.org.uk/news/dm2014-not-independent-without-standards-and-unorganised/.

of national and regional newspapers were exposed to a barrage of one-sided coverage of the issue, and invited to submit a standard response to the consultation, making the points that newspaper publishers wished them to make.[58]

When my father sent a letter criticising this campaign of misinformation to his local paper, the *York Press*, he was turned down for publication. The editor apparently preferred to run a simple diet of propaganda – in a newspaper which, as it happens, is owned by Newsquest, one of the largest newspaper companies in the UK and a leading member of the News Media Association, the newspaper lobbying organisation that co-ordinated the anti-Leveson campaign. Newsquest, in turn, is owned by Gannett, the largest newspaper company in the United States by circulation, with revenue of $3.1 billion in 2017.

Most industries try to avoid regulation, but the press has a unique capacity to push its agenda. More than 100,000 pro forma newspaper responses were received

---

58 For a selection of newspaper coverage of the issue, collated by the News Media Association, see http://www.newsmediauk.org/Free-the-Press-in-the-Media.

by the Department for Digital, Culture, Media and Sport (DCMS), which dutifully counted and included them in its consultation response – whilst discounting two online petitions signed by more than 200,000 people who were in favour of the Leveson reforms.[59] In 2018, the Secretary of State, Matt Hancock, went before the House of Commons and announced his decision not to go ahead with the Leveson reforms.[60] Even stranger than his refusal to count the consultation responses properly was his failure to read a letter from Sir Brian Leveson, who had written to say that he 'fundamentally' disagreed with the government's decision to scrap Part Two of his inquiry and that 'the bulk of Part Two [should] be commenced as soon as possible'.[61]

With a solemn face, the minister instead told the Commons that 'Sir Brian [...] agrees that the Inquiry should not proceed under the current terms of reference but believes that it should continue in an amended

---

59 See https://www.gov.uk/government/consultations/consultation-on-the-leveson-inquiry-and-its-implementation.

60 See https://www.gov.uk/government/speeches/leveson-consultation-response.

61 Available at https://www.gov.uk/government/consultations/consultation-on-the-leveson-inquiry-and-its-implementation.

form'. This description of Sir Brian's position was later challenged by Ian Lucas, an MP on the DCMS Select Committee, who asked why the Secretary of State had not acknowledged that Sir Brian 'fundamentally disagreed' with the government's conclusion. The minister could only stammer that he had 'explained Sir Brian's position in a way that is – I thought was straightforward'.[62]

Oddly enough, the minister's failure to explain himself to MPs was not covered in the press. The 'fourth estate' on this occasion were not particularly bothered about holding Hancock to account for misinforming the House of Commons. They had got what they wanted: a government commitment to protect them from independent scrutiny.

As the Leveson process went awry, I wondered – idly at first – whether it would be possible to establish a regulator that met the Leveson criteria for independent and effective regulation: a regulator unlike IPSO, which was

---

62 See http://data.parliament.uk/writtenevidence/committeeevidence.svc/
   evidencedocument/digital-culture-media-and-sport-committee/disinfor-
   mation-and-fake-news/oral/80607.html.

already compromised by its relationship with the newspaper publishers who controlled it. Many newspapers, magazines and websites were not planning to join IPSO. Would they welcome the prospect of an alternative?

I began talking to people about this. Many of them agreed that it was exactly what was needed. Executives at *The Guardian* did not want to be part of a regulator like IPSO that was set up and dominated by the publishers of the *Daily Mail* and *The Sun*. Nor did the publishers of many smaller newspapers and news websites. But no one wanted to take forward the task of setting up an alternative regulator.

I found the prospect oddly compelling, however, and I thought – naïvely, as it turned out – that with my background in journalism and press freedom campaigning, I could broker a consensus between different parts of the industry and civil society.

I came up with a name for the new regulator – IMPRESS: The Independent Monitor for the Press – and got to work. I received a start-up grant from the Joseph Rowntree Reform Trust and raised some more money through crowdfunding. I contacted Max Mosley and J. K. Rowling, both of whom had given evidence to the Leveson Inquiry about their experiences at the hands of the press.

Mosley is a motor racing entrepreneur whose sex life was exposed when the *News of the World* published a video of him taking part in a sadomasochistic sex party. Rowling is the author of the bestselling Harry Potter novels whose family was hounded by the press for years. She told the Leveson Inquiry that she was forced to hide her children under blankets when they left the house in order to stop paparazzi taking photographs of them. One day, she had brought her daughter home from school to find that a journalist had inserted a letter into her schoolbag.[63] Rowling and Mosley both agreed to support the initiative, as did a number of other individuals and foundations. However, their support brought challenges of its own.

J. K. Rowling may be a national treasure, but Max Mosley is one of the most controversial figures in British public life. He made his mark in the field of motor

---

63 See https://discoverleveson.com/hearing/2011-11-24/930/?bc=5.

racing, where, with his business partner Bernie Eccle-
stone, he developed Formula One into an international
sports empire. He also inherited money from his mother,
Diana Mitford, whose first husband was a member of
the Guinness family. His father, Oswald Mosley, was a
Labour politician in the 1920s who went on to form the
British Union of Fascists. The *News of the World* used
this family history to justify the exposure of Mosley's
sex life, claiming – wrongly, as it turned out – that participants in the sex party had been wearing Nazi costumes.

Mosley's background is a world away from my own.
Whilst Oswald Mosley was campaigning against immigration in the 1960s, my own father was working with
civil rights activists in the American South, helping black
citizens register to vote. He faced very real risks in the
fight against racism. He was a few miles away when three
fellow activists were murdered in Neshoba County,
Mississippi – the events memorialised in the film *Mississippi Burning*.

My political upbringing was on the left. Max Mosley's was on the right. And yet, when we first met, we
hit it off. His private life had been blown apart when the

News of the World splashed naked photographs of him on its front page. As he told me, he was lucky enough to be able to take on his intruders in the courts, where he won. But he knew that most people could not afford the cost of a libel or privacy action. So he wanted to see significant improvements in access to justice, through legal reforms and an improved system of press regulation. He had paid for many ordinary victims of phone hacking to have legal representation in the Leveson Inquiry, so that their voices could be heard. He now wanted to do more to help implement the Leveson reforms.

Mosley had set aside a certain amount of money for his son Alexander to inherit. However, Alexander had died of a drug overdose the year after his father's sex life was exposed. Now, Mosley wanted to do something purposeful with the money. He said that he would be prepared to underwrite the costs of IMPRESS until the organisation was self-sufficient.

It was an extremely generous offer, but I had to do something that is almost unheard of in fundraising. I had to tell Mosley that, whilst we would be grateful for his support, we would not welcome his involvement in the work of IMPRESS. We did not want him to get involved in appointing the IMPRESS board, writing its code or overseeing its regulatory decisions. We did not want to remove the control of the press barons only to allow a motor racing mogul to take their place.

Mosley completely agreed. He offered to set up a new charity to handle the funds, so that he would not be directly involved. He wished us well and accepted that in order for IMPRESS to succeed, it had to do things in its own way.

Some of my former associates were not best pleased with IMPRESS. My former *Observer* colleague Nick Cohen called IMPRESS supporters 'naïve' for daring to support independent press regulation.[64] 'Sinister zealots', screamed *The Sun*, above mugshots of me and other members of the IMPRESS team.[65] The *Daily Mail* linked my work with IMPRESS to an attempt – years earlier – to stand for election as a Labour councillor in the affluent London borough of Kensington and Chelsea:

---

64 Nick Cohen, 'J. K. Rowling is too good to be a propagandist', *The Observer*, 9 August 2014.

65 Oliver Harvey, 'Fight for right to tell truth', *The Sun*, 30 December 2016.

'He would not be representing the interests of the very famous and the very wealthy, at least not for quite a long time to come,' they jeered.[66] Jacob Rees-Mogg, a Conservative MP known as the 'Member of Parliament for the Eighteenth Century', linked me to Max Mosley's family history of racism.[67]

Water off a duck's back? Not really. But Rees-Mogg is protected by parliamentary privilege, and a complaint to IPSO would have been ridiculous. Other victims of press abuse warned me that the papers would only step up their attacks if I retaliated. In any case, I still believed that the papers had the right to publish a range of views on these issues.

I was disappointed, however, to find that the papers did not publish a range of views. They simply published a narrow, one-sided and highly distorted version of the facts, over and over again. Of 1,421 articles about press regulation published in the national press in the

---

66 Richard Pendlebury, 'How orgy-loving Max Mosley is using his millions to seek vengeance on the press', *Daily Mail*, 15 April 2016.

67 See https://hansard.parliament.uk/Commons/2018-03-05/debates/0343F7DB-6456-4448-B9B8-BA7A1FFCD01D/DataProtectionBill(Lords).

year following Leveson's report, a significant majority portrayed Leveson as a threat to press freedom.[68] In most national newspapers, fewer than one in five pieces about Leveson included a balance of positive and negative opinions. In some, the proportion of negative to positive coverage was overwhelming: there were twenty-nine negative pieces for every single positive piece in *The Sun*, and thirty-three in the *Daily Mail*. Most newspaper articles with an opinion portrayed Leveson's recommendations as a threat to press freedom. 'Crackdown that could stifle your right to know,' said the *Daily Mail* (30 November 2012); 'Lords a-leaping to gag the press,' said the *Sunday Times* (10 February 2013); 'A muzzled media will make victims of us all,' said the *Daily Telegraph* (18 March 2013); 'A dire day for freedom,' said the *Daily Mirror* (9 October 2013).

Nobody was left in any doubt about what these newspapers thought about regulation.

---

68 Gordon Neil Ramsay, 'How Newspapers Covered Press Regulation After Leveson', op. cit.

The revenge of the journalists

Five years later, and the press are singing a very different tune. Having argued for decades that any form of regulation is anathema to media freedom, they have begun to call for a tough new form of regulation. Not for themselves, but for the social media companies that are having a devastating impact on their audiences – and their finances.

In the years since the Leveson Inquiry, newspapers sometimes mentioned the rise of the social media industry as a sign that Leveson was out of touch with the modern world. However, they did not offer any proposals of their own to deal with the digital media revolution. I once mentioned this to a senior journalist, who laughed that trying to regulate the internet would be as vain as asking Canute to turn back the tide.

And then, in 2017, newspapers woke up to the existential threat posed by social media. As it happens, this was around the time that Facebook began to outstrip newspapers as a source of news, and the share of the UK advertising market controlled by internet companies soared above 50 per cent.[69] Suddenly, the new media giants were threatening the one thing that newspaper owners value more than press freedom itself: their business model. The *Telegraph* called for statutory regulation.[70] *The Independent* said that any new social media regulator should 'answer directly to the government'.[71] The *Daily Mail* urged the government to 'stand up to these utterly unscrupulous multinational leviathans'.[72] And *The Guardian* declared that Facebook was 'long overdue a regulatory reckoning'.[73]

Statutory regulation? A regulator answering directly to the government? Unscrupulous multinational leviathans?!

---

69 See https://www.pewresearch.org/fact-tank/2018/12/10/social-media-out-paces-print-newspapers-in-the-u-s-as-a-news-source/; and Stephen Adshead, Grant Forsyth, Sam Wood and Laura Wilkinson, 'Online advertising in the UK' (London: Department for Digital, Culture, Media and Sport, January 2019), p. 35.

70 Charles Hymas, 'Government draws up plans for social media regulator following Telegraph campaign', *Daily Telegraph*, 20 September 2018.

71 'The Molly Russell case is yet more evidence of urgent need for social media regulation', *The Independent*, 27 January 2019.

72 Stephen Glover, 'The press CAN thrive online if we stand up to these digital leviathans', *Daily Mail*, 12 February 2019.

73 'The Guardian view on Zuckerberg's Facebook: regulate it as a media firm', *The Guardian*, 28 November 2018.

What sinister zealots are these, who dare to suggest that politicians should play any part in regulating the media? As it happens, they are the same newspaper companies that spent the better part of a decade fighting tooth and nail against independent regulation of their own behaviour. One or two of them might even be described as multinational leviathans, though they would blush to hear it.

The media commentator Emily Bell has dubbed this phenomenon 'the revenge of the journalists'.[74] At the same time as continuing to campaign against the post-Leveson framework – sometimes even in the same breath – newspapers have been calling for tougher regulation of the social media platforms that are rocking their world. They are saying that new media companies *must not* be free to provide a platform for fake news – or the truth will suffer. Social media companies *must not* be free from democratic oversight – or they will

---

74 See Jonathan Heawood, 'Independent publishers are getting left behind as "big beasts" use latest tech tools to "game" online platforms', *Press Gazette*, 6 June 2018, available at https://www.pressgazette.co.uk/independent-publishers-are-getting-left-behind-as-big-beasts-use-latest-tech-tools-to-game-online-platforms/4/.

distort democracy. Social media companies *must not* be free to provide a platform for whatever content they like – or people will be harmed. Their position may be inconsistent, but their demands have been effective, and lawmakers have leaped into action to propose a new regulator for social media.

How can newspapers be so strongly in favour of regulation of social media and yet so vehemently opposed to regulation of the press? Do they seriously think that freedom should apply to them but not their competitors? Could they be right? Is there some fundamental difference between old and new media which means that newspapers deserve more freedom than social media platforms? If so, what exactly is the difference?

Part III

Part III

Breaking Press Freedom

I N 2004, A young man called Mark Zuckerberg
created a platform for his fellow Harvard under-
graduates to rate each other's sexual allure. He
posted images of each student's face from their academic
yearbook and let adolescent lust do the rest.

Fifteen years later, and Zuckerberg's dorm room
exploits have turned Facebook into a global empire
that sits alongside Google, Amazon and Apple as one
of the biggest companies in the history of the planet.[75] These firms operate different services in different
ways, but together, they act as gatekeepers to the world's

---

75 'Silicon Valley and the state gird for war', *The Economist*, 5 October 2019.
    See *Digital Dominance: The Power of Google, Amazon, Facebook, and Apple*,
    ed. Martin Moore and Damian Tambini (Oxford: Oxford University Press,
    2018) on the impact of these companies on a range of markets.

information, enabling human beings across the globe to communicate in radically new ways. Where once we were passive consumers of the media, we are now active participants in its creation. We can self-publish our books through Amazon, our videos through You-Tube and our photographs through Facebook and its subsidiaries, WhatsApp and Instagram.

The relationship between social media platforms and their users is radically different from the relationship between old media companies and their audiences. Now, ordinary people can speak in their own voice, unmediated by newspapers, broadcasters or professional politicians. We can argue directly with each other on topics from immigration to gun control, from abortion to Israel. The old gatekeepers' control over moral and political discourse has broken down, with effects that are still unravelling before our eyes.

This should be a golden age for media freedom. However, there is a dark side to the new public sphere. For this flowering of alternative voices is in the gift of gargantuan tech companies that can decide which individuals and which news sources to place at the heart of the debate and which to push to the margins. These media giants are ultimately no more innocent than their forebears in the press. As corporations, they are not innately interested in truth, democracy or self-expression. They are interested in a business model that demands our attention, and our data. In developing this business model, they have exposed some uncomfortable aspects of human behaviour – aspects that press freedom fundamentalists would rather ignore.

Truth and social media

The birth of printing helped to establish modern science. When scholars in different countries were first able to communicate swiftly and openly with each other, they could share evidence proving that the sun does not orbit the earth and that the earth is not at the centre of the universe. These facts became so universally accepted that to doubt them was a sign of eccentricity or even madness. A 'Flat Earther' (or geoplanarian) is the dictionary definition of someone who does not accept the realities of modern life.

But now Flat Earthers are on the rise. According to a poll in 2018, only 84 per cent of Americans are entirely confident that the earth is spherical.[76] This figure drops to just 66 per cent among 18–24-year-olds. In other words, *one-third of young Americans are not sure that the world is round*. They may not be out-and-out Flat Earthers, but they have serious doubts about what they call 'Globalism' (or what the rest of us call *the truth*).

What is causing these young people to reject hundreds of years of science? According to some researchers, it is YouTube. Flat Earthers have racked up considerable online support among celebrity YouTubers such as Logan Paul, who has more than 18 million followers and who came out of the closet as a Flat Earther in 2018.[77] Researchers found that delegates at Flat Earth

---

76 See https://today.yougov.com/topics/philosophy/articles-reports/2018/04/02/most-flat-earthers-consider-themselves-religious.

77 Josiah Hesse, 'Flat Earthers keep the faith at Denver conference', *The Guardian*, 18 November 2018.

conventions had been converted to the Flat Earth theory after watching YouTube:

> Most had been watching videos about other conspiracies, with alternative takes on 9/11, the Sandy Hook school shooting and whether Nasa really went to the moon, when YouTube offered up Flat Earth videos for them to watch next. Some said they watched the videos only in order to debunk them but soon found themselves won over by the material.[78]

Social media algorithms are programmed to serve up content that caters to your taste. If you watch a lot of videos about kittens, YouTube gives you videos about puppies. If you watch videos saying that high school shootings have been staged, then you will soon be seeing videos telling you the earth is flat.

In a bizarre irony, some Facebook workers have even come to believe in the conspiracy theories they

---

78 Ian Sample, 'Study blames YouTube for rise in number of Flat Earthers', *The Guardian*, 17 February 2019.

are supposed to be monitoring. Early in 2019, a reporter from The Verge interviewed a dozen current and former employees of a company that provides moderation services for social media platforms. They described a surreal working environment:

> ... a place where the conspiracy videos and memes that they see each day gradually lead them to embrace fringe views. One auditor walks the floor promoting the idea that the Earth is flat. A former employee told me he has begun to question certain aspects of the Holocaust. Another former employee, who told me he has mapped every escape route out of his house and sleeps with a gun at his side, said: 'I no longer believe 9/11 was a terrorist attack.'[79]

You do not have to read this stuff for a living to be influenced by it. One study has found that 60 per cent of

---

79 Casey Newton, 'The trauma floor: the secret lives of Facebook moderators in America', The Verge, 25 February 2019, available at https://www.theverge.com/2019/2/25/18229714/cognizant-facebook-content-moderator-interviews-trauma-working-conditions-arizona.

British people now believe at least one conspiracy theory.[80] Popular theories maintain that the government is hiding the truth about how many immigrants really live in the country; that immigration is part of a bigger plan to make Muslims a majority of the country's population; and that the idea of man-made climate change is a hoax. One of the most popular theories currently doing the rounds is the anti-vaccination, or 'anti-vaxx', theory. Ten per cent of Britons and 15 per cent of Americans now believe that 'the truth about the harmful effects of vaccines is being deliberately hidden from the public'.[81]

Of course, there is something counter-intuitive about sticking a needle full of disease into your body in order to avoid an infection. Early critics even feared that the smallpox vaccine would turn you into a cow. Modern-day

---

80 Esther Addley, 'Study shows 60% of Britons believe in conspiracy theories', *The Guardian*, 23 November 2018. This study defines a conspiracy theory as 'a theory that some actors have conspired to do something covertly, usually something dysfunctional or evil'. For the full results, see https://d25d2506s-fb94s.cloudfront.net/cumulus_uploads/document/pk1qbgil4c/YGC%20 Conspiracy%20Theories%20(all%20countries).pdf.

81 Ibid.

anti-vaxxers do not share this particular belief, but they are seizing on the work of maverick scientists and alternative health practitioners to spread fear about the consequences of everyday vaccines. The reinforcing cycle of conspiracy theories on YouTube and other social media platforms has created an epidemic of anti-vaxxing. A report by the Royal Society for Public Health showed that half of new parents in the UK are now exposed to anti-vaccine misinformation on social media.[82] Vaccination rates have gone down, infection rates have gone up, and measles cases in Europe have risen to their highest level for twenty years.[83] Alarmed by the return of diseases that had been stamped out in Europe and North America, the World Health Organization is redirecting precious resources to the anti-vaxxing panic.

How does misinformation find its way to parents on social media? One explanation is innocent enough.

---

82 'Moving the Needle: Promoting vaccination uptake across the life course' (Royal Society for Public Health, 2018), p. 12, available at https://www.rsph.org.uk/our-work/policy/vaccinations/moving-the-needle-promoting-vaccination-uptake-across-the-life-course.html.

83 Sarah Boseley, 'Measles cases at highest for 20 years in Europe, as anti-vaccine movement grows', *The Guardian*, 21 December 2018.

Your family and friends see something about the dangers of a particular vaccine. They share it with you, you share it with your friends, and so it goes on, gathering attention as it travels around the web. However, there is also something darker at work here. Early in 2019, reporters at *The Guardian* discovered that Facebook was enabling advertisers to promote content to nearly 900,000 people who had been identified by the platform as interested in 'vaccine controversies'.[84] These advertisers include groups who, against medical advice, sell vitamin supplements as an alternative to vaccinations.[85] By harvesting data on its users, and then packaging and selling those users to advertisers, Facebook is building a bridge between people who want to protect their children but are ignorant about medical science, and people who want to exploit that ignorance to sell things. This would be bad enough if the anti-vaxxers were only affecting their own family's health. But they are not. By

84 Julia Carrie Wong, 'Revealed: Facebook enables ads to target users interested in "vaccine controversies"', *The Guardian*, 15 February 2019.

85 Ed Pilkington and Jessica Glenza, 'Facebook under pressure to halt rise of anti-vaccination groups', *The Guardian*, 12 February 2019.

failing to vaccinate their own children, they are endangering other children, particularly babies who have not yet reached the vaccination age. As a spokesperson for the American Academy of Pediatrics has said, 'This isn't just self-harm, it's community harm.'[86]

Wasn't the marketplace of ideas supposed to stamp out falsehoods and replace them with the truth? Well, there is no shortage of accurate information out there on the internet, but the falsehoods keep on spreading. Some of the most popular fake stories on Facebook in 2018 included the following:

- 'Woman sues Samsung for $1.8m after cell phone gets stuck inside her vagina';
- 'Donald Trump ends school shootings by banning schools'; and
- 'Florida man arrested for tranquilizing and raping alligators in Everglades'.[87]

---

86 Ibid.
87 Craig Silverman and Scott Pham, 'These Are 50 Of The Biggest Fake News Hits On Facebook In 2018', BuzzFeed, 28 December 2018, available at https://www.buzzfeednews.com/article/craigsilverman/facebook-fake-news-hits-2018.

These headlines are so obviously absurd that we struggle to imagine how anyone could ever believe them. Nonetheless, people have believed – and acted on – even more extraordinary claims.

In autumn 2016, rumours surfaced on social media that Hillary Clinton was running a child sexual exploitation ring out of a pizzeria in downtown Washington DC. Most people would shake their heads at this, or expect the FBI to investigate the claims. However, many online users believed what they read, and – because they were already inclined to mistrust the government – they did not expect the 'feds' to deal with a conspiracy in such high places. One young man took matters into his own hands, and, on 4 December, Edgar Maddison Welch entered the pizzeria with an assault rifle and fired shots into the walls, a desk and a door. No one was hurt, but things could have been very different. Welch later told police that he had read about the exploitation ring online and wanted to do something about it. Even after his arrest, some conspiracy theorists refused to let go of their belief in 'Pizzagate', preferring to believe that the shooting *itself* had been staged in order to divert attention away from the real wrongdoers.

How can so many people be so wrong about so many things, so much of the time? Well, the prevalence of misinformation (accidental falsehoods) and disinformation (deliberate falsehoods) on social media has inspired some fascinating research into the way humans process information. This research has implications not only for our understanding of fake news on social media, but also for how we think about press freedom in general.

It turns out that we are *all* at risk of falling for fake news, not because we have gone mad, but because of two quite normal features of the human mind: information cascades and confirmation bias.

We may not believe everything we read – at least, not at first. However, when a false message is repeated enough times, people start to credit it – even when (like the Flat Earthers) they began by being sure that it was a lie.[88] As the Royal Society for Public Health puts it, 'Substantial exposure to negative vaccination messages may influence attitudes to vaccinations over time:

---

88 Lisa K. Fazio, Nadia M. Brashier, B. Keith Payne, Elizabeth J. Marsh, 'Knowledge Does Not Protect Against Illusory Truth', *Journal of Experimental Psychology*, Vol. 144, No. 5 (2015), 993–1002.

repetition of messages is often mistaken for accuracy.'[89] People copy other people's choices rather than reaching their own independent conclusions. You do not have to be mad to believe what other people believe. In fact, this is normally the mark of sanity. Ten thousand years ago, if someone told us that a sabre-toothed tiger was heading our way, we quickly passed on the information, without stopping to verify whether or not our informant had actually seen the beast in question. In that context, this way of sharing information was perfectly sensible. In a changed context, it can spread fake news around the world in seconds.

Social media platforms and search engines exaggerate information cascades, because they generate results that flow from your existing interests and preferences. *If you like that conspiracy theory, you'll love this one! If you believe that Barack Obama was born in Kenya, you'll be fascinated to learn that Osama bin Laden is alive and well and living in Washington DC!* In 2011, the online activist Eli Pariser coined the term 'filter bubble' to

---

89 'Moving the Needle', op. cit., p. 12.

define the self-fulfilling universe in which some internet users reside.[90] Whilst more recent research has challenged some of Pariser's assumptions (by showing that readers of online news are actually consuming *more* sources of information than they would have done in the offline world), this does not change the underlying problem: that our predisposition to believe what other people believe leaves us ill-equipped to make our way through a vast online marketplace of ideas.

John Milton imagined his audience as intellectual pilgrims, seriously searching for the truth. Such wayfarers (if they existed) might be committed to what social psychologists call *exploratory* thought – an 'evenhanded consideration of alternative points of view'.[91] Science and law proceed on the basis of exploratory thought.

---

90 See Eli Pariser, *The Filter Bubble: What the Internet Is Hiding from You* (London: Penguin, 2011).

91 J. S. Lerner and P. E. Tetlock, 'Bridging individual, interpersonal, and institutional approaches to judgment and decision making: The impact of accountability on cognitive bias', in *Emerging Perspectives on Judgment and Decision Research*, ed. S. L. Schneider and J. Shanteau (New York, NY: Cambridge University Press, 2003), pp. 431–57, cited in Jonathan Haidt, *The Righteous Mind: Why Good People Are Divided by Politics and Religion* (London: Allen Lane, 2012), p. 88.

Evidence is tested and debated until some kind of agreed truth emerges. Science and law are not perfect, by any stretch of the imagination, but they do at least mitigate our susceptibility to information cascades.

Much of the time, however, we are engaged in *confirmatory* thought – 'a one-sided attempt to rationalise a particular point of view'.[92] In this mode, we seek out sources of information (friends, neighbours, newspapers, websites) that confirm what we already believe. If we think that immigration is good for society, then we seize on stories that highlight the positive contribution made by immigrants and ignore the evidence to the contrary. Conversely, if we are predisposed against immigration, we gobble up stories about crime and community tension and ignore the stories about economic and cultural benefits. Most of us, much of the time, simply turn a blind eye to information that challenges our preconceptions. We are not interested in the 'truth' about immigration. We are not dispassionate shoppers in the marketplace of ideas. We do not even-handedly consider alternative points of view.

---

92 Ibid.

This confirmation bias means that our brains are often more interested in information that is *useful* to us (by reinforcing our prior beliefs) than in information that is *truthful*.[93] We get hold of the facts that suit us and ignore the ones that do not. Even if the truth is out there, we might not see it. Even worse, we might see it but reject it, simply because we have seen other people reject it.

For a religious believer like John Milton, truth was a function of faith. Get your faith right, and the truth would follow. For a rationalist like John Stuart Mill, the truth was a function of the facts. Get the facts right, and the truth would follow. Milton and Mill were wrong. When truth and falsehood grapple, there is no guarantee that truth will win. Falsehood, by its nature, plays dirty, whilst the truth is tragically honourable.

Self-expression and social media

John Stuart Mill wanted everyone to be free to express themselves. He thought that, by developing our talents

---

93 See Rob Brotherton, *Suspicious Minds: Why We Believe Conspiracy Theories* (London: Bloomsbury, 2015).

in this way, we would become more useful to ourselves and our communities. There are large parts of the internet in which Mill's dream is a happy reality – platforms that have enabled artists, makers and technicians to share their work with new audiences, and where amateurs and professionals meet and mingle, leading to cross-fertilisation and exciting hybrids.

Social media has also enabled people who were once isolated to reach out and hold one another's hands. They have built communities – online groups that have transformed their lives and the lives of their societies. These groups have addressed the stigma that once left people leading lives of quiet misery. They have given a voice to the voiceless. No longer defined by the gatekeepers of the old media, these vulnerable groups can speak for themselves, enjoying a level of self-expression that previous generations could only dream of. As a result, there has been a flowering of alternative identities, as people break free from the roles that defined them for centuries.

At the same time, social media has proved to be a fertile ground for a turbo-charged form of identity politics. Some platforms have developed a profile as forums for harassment, abuse and trolling. Twitter, in particular, suffers from this reputation. The combination of pithy messages with an argumentative culture has turned Twitter into the so-called amygdala of the internet – a place where the most primitive aspects of the human brain run riot.[94] Twitter users experience a raised pulse, enlarged pupils and sweating when they are on the site.[95] Simply browsing your Twitter feed increases emotional arousal by 65 per cent, and actively tweeting and retweeting raises it by 75 per cent. This makes Twitter users more prone to responding to perceived threats with a 'fight or flight' reaction, driven by the amygdala, rather than a more considered or compassionate response.

Twitter is a particularly threatening place for people in the public eye who are obliged to use the platform to engage with their constituents. It is worse for women than men, and it is worst of all for women from black and minority ethnic backgrounds. Research by Amnesty International has shown that 7 per cent of the tweets directed at

---

94 Tali Sharot, *The Influential Mind: What the Brain Reveals About Our Power to Change Others* (London: Little, Brown, 2017), pp. 48–51.
95 Ibid., p. 49.

female journalists and politicians are abusive.[96] This rises to 10 per cent of tweets directed at prominent black women. This may not sound too bad, until you take into account the high volume of tweets involved. The MP Diane Abbott received *more than 8,000 abusive tweets* in a six-week period alone.[97] Examples included the following:

- 'this fat retarded black bitch thinks you should be forced to feed and house a bunch of violence [*sic*] foreign invaders. i strongly disagree.'
- 'Piss off you disgusting useless fat bitch! You're a parasite alien looking to silence native people for your power.'
- 'An acid attack would probably make your face look better you fat n****r.'[98]

---

96 Amnesty International, 'Troll Patrol Findings: Using Crowdsourcing, Data Science & Machine Learning to Measure Violence and Abuse against Women on Twitter', available at https://decoders.amnesty.org/projects/troll-patrol/findings.

97 Azmina Dhrodia, 'Unsocial Media: Tracking Twitter Abuse against Women MPs', Medium, 4 September 2017, available at https://medium.com/@AmnestyInsights/unsocial-media-tracking-twitter-abuse-against-women-mps-fc28aeca498a.

98 All quoted in Azmina Dhrodia, 'Unsocial Media', ibid.

Abbott told Amnesty that the first thing her staff have to do every morning is 'go online and delete and block all the stuff'.[99] She believes that the abuse she receives would make 'younger women of colour very hesitant about entering the public debate and thinking about going into politics'.[100]

The social media economy has exposed, exploited and exacerbated uncomfortable truths about human behaviour. We are emotional animals. Our reasoning ability is easily hijacked by emotional triggers that lure us into harmful behaviour – shooting off tweets that seek to degrade other people's standing. The press freedom myth has aided this phenomenon, by proclaiming that the media is synonymous with self-expression, and that self-expression is supremely important. In publishing and defending the views of their star columnists, some national newspapers have been normalising abusive speech for decades.

In a recent report, the Committee on Standards in

---

99 Damien Gayle, 'Diane Abbott: Twitter has "put racists into overdrive"', *The Guardian*, 18 December 2018.

100 Azmina Dhrodia, 'Unsocial Media', op. cit.

Public Life charted an ecosystem of abuse, whereby attacks on public figures circulate between old and new media. When abuse starts on social media, the committee noted that 'the traditional press and broadcast media can trigger and perpetuate ... "tweet storms" by reporting on them'.[101] At the same time, the committee called on journalists, broadcasters and editors to 'consider whether the content they are creating could incite others to engage in intimidatory behaviour'.[102]

As an example, the committee cited a front page of the *Daily Telegraph* that denounced fifteen Conservative MPs as 'mutineers' because of their position on Brexit.[103] One of those named by the *Telegraph* – Anna Soubry – subsequently told the House of Commons that she had received a number of threatening tweets which her office had reported to the police. She called on the Speaker to 'make it very clear to everybody, in whatever capacity, that they have an absolute duty to

---

101 Committee on Standards in Public Life, 'Intimidation in Public Life' (London: Her Majesty's Stationery Office, December 2017), p. 39.

102 Ibid., p. 74.

103 'The Brexit mutineers: At least 15 Tory MPs rebel against leave date with threat to join forces with Labour', *Daily Telegraph*, 15 November 2017.

report responsibly … and to make sure that we have a democracy that welcomes free speech and an attitude of tolerance'.[104]

I have succumbed to the amygdala of the internet myself, posting a series of tweets and retweets that attacked the *Daily Mail* and *The Sun* over their coverage of the Brexit debate and immigration. I realised, too late, that I had gone too far, and apologised and deleted my Twitter account.[105] For me, the costs of being on Twitter far outweighed the benefits, but for many others, it remains the dominant forum for political and personal debate. Every day, millions of people go online in order to express their views, and shout down the views of others.

Tiring, isn't it? And where is it getting any of us? Is it helping us to realise our potential as human beings? Or are we simply helping the owners and shareholders

---

104 See https://hansard.parliament.uk/Commons/2017-11-15/debates/F52A07EF-C782-4773-85AD-1C0E2624AAA5/PointsOfOrder.

105 See Jonathan Heawood, 'Impress chief exec: "I let the side down with ill-judged tweets aimed at Sun and Mail"', *Press Gazette*, 29 September 2017, available at https://www.pressgazette.co.uk/impress-chief-i-let-the-side-down-with-ill-judged-tweets-aimed-at-sun-and-mail/.

of Twitter, Facebook and YouTube to realise huge profit margins – at the expense, ultimately, of our own capacity for meaningful self-expression?

Worst of all, are we actually serving the cause of those who want to shut down democracy altogether?

Democracy and social media

In 2011, pro-democracy protests in Tunisia spread rapidly across other Arab countries in North Africa and the Middle East, thanks in part to the connective tissue of social media. Free from the political control that had long threatened dissidents in the old media, individual users were able to share messages on Facebook and Twitter, helping a huge popular movement to make demands for change. It felt like a tipping point. The old gatekeepers were dead! No longer would political discourse be controlled by politicians and press barons. Now, the people could speak to and for each other. Together, we would change the world.

Those months in 2011 may have been the high point for social media as an engine of democracy. No sooner had the protests flared up across the Arab world than they were swept away. In Syria, a pro-democracy uprising turned into an horrific civil war, and political reforms in Tunisia and Egypt were swiftly reversed. In many other Arab countries, it is as though spring never came.

Since the Arab Spring, there has been a steady stream of allegations that social media, far from expanding political participation, has the potential to undermine democracy. Platforms, like internet service providers (ISPs), gather huge amounts of data on their users. They are under pressure to share that data with governments, at home and abroad. In 2013, Edward Snowden published a wealth of information garnered from his time at the National Security Agency which showed that intelligence agencies in the US and the UK were working with ISPs to open the 'backdoor' to the internet, by deliberately weakening the encryption systems that keep our messages private.[106] As a result, vast amounts of private communications were exposed to scrutiny by spies

---

106 See James Ball, Julian Borger and Glenn Greenwald, 'Revealed: how US and UK spy agencies defeat internet privacy and security', *The Guardian*, 6 September 2013.

on both sides of the Atlantic. As if that were not bad enough, some platforms are also available for governments and other political forces to spread propaganda – not, as they once did, through public channels such as television broadcasts and billboard posters, but by targeting individual citizens directly.

In a series of articles published in *The Observer* between 2017 and 2018, Carole Cadwalladr revealed that a firm called Cambridge Analytica had used the personal data of about 200,000 Facebook users to build up detailed psychological profiles of *87 million* Facebook users.[107] Whilst the initial 200,000 users had voluntarily completed an online personality quiz, they had not known how their answers would be used. The 87 million users who were profiled had most certainly not given their informed consent.

Cambridge Analytica used this massive database to help political campaigners in the United Kingdom, the

---

107 See Carole Cadwalladr and Emma Graham-Harrison, 'Revealed: 50 million Facebook profiles harvested for Cambridge Analytica in major data breach', *The Guardian*, 17 March 2018; and Martin Moore, *Democracy Hacked: Political Turmoil and Information Warfare in the Digital Age* (London: Oneworld, 2018).

United States and other countries target Facebook users with highly specific messages.

Facebook initially tried to deny all responsibility for this use of their platform. However, it soon became clear that not only was Facebook highly vulnerable to abuse; it had actively promoted its capacity to target users in this way.[108] Targeted advertising is, in fact, at the heart of Facebook's business model. Like other social media platforms and search engines, Facebook attracts users to its 'free' service. However, it collects data on every user and their actions, allowing the company to build up incredibly detailed profiles of each of us, which it sells to advertisers. We, the users, are not Facebook's customers. We are its product.

Ever since the Cambridge Analytica scandal, Facebook has been in damage-limitation mode, plastering adverts all over London, Brussels and Washington assuring policymakers that 'fake news is not our friend'. There is something oddly innocent about this campaign

---

108 Martin Moore, *Democracy Hacked*, ibid., pp. 107–35.

– in stark contrast to the highly sophisticated form of advertising that Facebook provides for its customers.

Microtargeting has been defined as 'a type of personalised communication that involves collecting information about people, and using that information to show them targeted political advertisements'.[109] Cambridge Analytica used a profiling tool called OCEAN to categorise Facebook users on the basis of their 'openness', 'conscientiousness', 'extroversion', 'agreeableness' and 'neuroticism'. How did they deduce these traits? Through an extensive and intrusive analysis of people's posts and interactions with other users.

They then helped their clients to target users with the most effective messages. For example, Cambridge Analytica 'might play on the fears of someone who could be frightened into believing that they needed the right to have a gun to protect their home from intruders'.[110]

---

109 Frederik J. Zuiderveen Borgesius, Judith Möller, Sanne Kruikemeier, Ronan Ó. Fathaigh, Kristina Irion, Tom Dobber, Balazs Bodo, Claes de Vreese, 'Online Political Microtargeting: Promises and Threats for Democracy', *Utrecht Law Review*, Vol. 14, No. 1 (2018), 82–96.

110 House of Commons Digital, Culture, Media and Sport Committee, 'Disinformation and "fake news": Interim Report' (July 2018), p. 28.

The House of Commons Select Committee on Digital, Culture, Media and Sport has concluded that this 'relentless targeting of hyper-partisan views, which play to the fears and the prejudices of people, in order to alter their voting plans', is arguably 'more invasive than obviously false information'. The committee describes the combined impact of misinformation and microtargeting as a 'democratic crisis'.[111]

In its early days, the internet looked like a democratising technology. To some extent, it has realised that potential. Nobody with an internet connection need ever feel alone again. Even if you are only one in a million, there are thousands of you in the world, and you can get together online. Movements like #BlackLivesMatter and #MeToo would not have been possible before social media. The simple use of a hashtag to aggregate messages has given voice to the voiceless, emboldening individual victims of abuse and discrimination to come together and lobby for change on a massive scale.

However, these tools are also available to the powerful.

---

111 Ibid., pp. 3, 26, 51.

The Cambridge Analytica scandal has shown quite how far social media has been penetrated by corporations and politicians who were far from voiceless in the first place. We now know that groups such as the Russian Internet Research Agency have used social media to create thousands or maybe millions of robot accounts ('bots'), pumping out automated propaganda to an unsuspecting world.[112]

These bots have colonised genuine online movements and created new ones. In the United States, they acted in support of the election of Donald Trump, but they have also appeared in association with liberal campaigns against racism and in favour of abortion. In one example, Russian bots were the driving force behind two rival protest groups in small-town Texas.[113] These bots fed on social media's bias towards attention-grabbing content

---

112 See Charles Maynes, 'The trolls are winning, says Russian troll hunter', Public Radio International, 13 March 2019, available at https://www.pri.org/stories/2019-03-13/trolls-are-winning-says-russian-troll-hunter.

113 Claire Allbright, 'A Russian Facebook page organized a protest in Texas. A different Russian page launched the counterprotest', *Texas Tribune*, 1 November 2017, available at https://www.texastribune.org/2017/11/01/russian-facebook-page-organized-protest-texas-different-russian-page-l/.

to generate viral activity, and drew real Facebook users towards their artificial campaigns, leaving discord and division in their wake. Their hand has also been revealed behind online culture wars across Europe and North America.[114] Without leaving the comfort of their desks in St Petersburg, Russian operatives can plant outrage in the hearts of ordinary internet users, adding to the climate of hostility and polarisation that now characterises political discourse around the world.

The digital economy has given us the prospect of a genuinely democratic media, free from the control of the old gatekeepers. At the same time, it has empowered a new global elite: the owners of the platforms, and the political and commercial advertisers who use this unregulated space to spread misinformation, exploiting our attraction towards sensationalist content that confirms our worst fears. This is not democracy. This is not helping us to make decisions on the basis of the facts. This is chaos.

---

114 See https://securingdemocracy.gmfus.org/.

A regulatory reckoning

Nicolas Sarkozy was one of the first world leaders to challenge the *laissez-faire* lions of the west coast, as criticisms of social media began to gain force in 2011. As President of France, he summoned them to Paris to account for themselves. Mark Zuckerberg, the founder and CEO of Facebook, pushed back against Sarkozy's call for regulation:

> People tell me: 'It's great you played such a big role in the Arab Spring, but it's also kind of scary because you enable all this sharing and collect information on people.' But it's hard to have one without the other. You can't isolate some things you like about the internet and control other things that you don't.[115]

This was the kind of talk that led people to mock the very idea of internet regulation as a vain attempt to turn back the tide. We have come a long way since then. Now, some of the most powerful people in social media are rebelling against the monstrous aspects of what they

---

115 'Zuckerberg and Schmidt warn on over-regulation of web', BBC News, 25 May 2011, available at https://www.bbc.co.uk/news/technology-13553943.

have created. In November 2017, one of Facebook's first investors publicly distanced himself from the platform. Describing himself as a 'conscientious objector', Sean Parker said that Facebook exploits psychological vulnerabilities to encourage users to become addicted to the site.[116] The following month, a former Facebook executive accused the site of 'ripping apart the social fabric'.[117] In 2015, the CEO of Twitter, Dick Costolo, admitted frankly that 'we suck at dealing with abuse and trolls on the platform and we've sucked at it for years'.[118] In February 2019, Jack Dorsey, the founder of Twitter, gave himself a 'C' for social responsibility.[119]

116 Thuy Ong, 'Sean Parker on Facebook: "God only knows what it's doing to our children's brains"', The Verge, 9 November 2017, available at https://www.theverge.com/2017/11/9/16627724/sean-parker-facebook-childrens-brains-feedback-loop.

117 James Vincent, 'Former Facebook exec says social media is ripping apart society', The Verge, 11 December 2017, available at https://www.theverge.com/2017/12/11/16761016/former-facebook-exec-ripping-apart-society.

118 Nitasha Tiku and Casey Newton, 'Twitter CEO: "We suck at dealing with abuse"', The Verge, 4 February 2015, available at https://www.theverge.com/2015/2/4/7982099/twitter-ceo-sent-memo-taking-personal-responsibility-for-the.

119 See Tom McKay, 'Twitter CEO Jack Dorsey: I Suck and the Problem Is the Whole Site', Gizmodo, 12 February 2019, available at https://gizmodo.com/twitter-ceo-jack-dorsey-i-suck-and-the-problem-is-the-1832578727.

Newspapers have successfully put pressure on the platforms to clean up their act, and Facebook, Twitter and YouTube are now scrambling to install in-house compliance mechanisms: vast teams of fact-checkers and content moderators who are supposed to respond swiftly to any content that breaches their community guidelines.

We are increasingly aware of the abuses that are built into the social media economy – so much so, in fact, that the big platforms are at risk of lurching from libertarianism to censorship. In order to protect their brands, they will rush to take down content that might provoke outrage – content like the famous photograph of a naked girl fleeing a napalm attack during the Vietnam War. Facebook removed this photograph on the basis that it was a sexual image of a child – despite the fact that it is one of the most iconic photographs of the twentieth century, used to defend the rights of children around the world.[120]

---

120 See Tarleton Gillespie, *Custodians of the Internet: Platforms, content moderation, and the hidden decisions that shape social media* (London: Yale University Press, 2018).

This kind of botched attempt at compliance suggests that social media companies might not be the best people to strike the right balance between self-expression and harm, or to protect the rules of democracy. Clearly, unregulated platforms risk becoming a free-for-all of fake news, hate speech and micro-targeting. But platforms that regulate themselves run the equal and opposite risk of shutting out marginal voices. The challenge is to ensure that regulation genuinely respects the public interest. We need a media that is not only free from political control but that also helps us to find out the truth (rather than confirming our prejudices), express ourselves freely (whilst allowing others to express themselves as well) and hold the powerful to account (rather than exposing ourselves to covert propaganda, or giving up our innermost thoughts and feelings to the scrutiny of corporations and governments).

The best kinds of journalism once fulfilled these roles. But the social media revolution has swept them aside. In the United States, the newspaper industry lost $1.3 billion worth of editors' and reporters' jobs in a decade, and has shed 60 per cent of its workforce since 2000.[121] In the UK, more than 200 local newspapers have closed since 2005; the number of regional journalists has halved; and 58 per cent of the country does not have a dedicated local newspaper.[122] Social media platforms and search engines have taken the advertising revenue that once supported public interest journalism, but have not yet put anything sustainable in its place.

Newspaper owners were happy to boast of their freedom – so long as they were economically and politically dominant. Now that their business model is collapsing, they are looking to the state for help. Regional newspaper groups are taking hand-outs from the BBC to employ 'local democracy reporters', whilst the national press demands regulation for social media.

The press freedom myth tells us that the state always poses a threat to the media. It does not tell us what to do when the media is posing a threat to society, or when

---

121 Jill Abramson, *Merchants of Truth: Inside the News Revolution* (London: Bodley Head, 2019), p. 2.

122 Alice Hutton, 'The death of the local newspaper?', BBC News, 20 February 2018, available at https://www.bbc.co.uk/news/uk-43106436.

different parts of the media are destroying each other. In order to deal with these new challenges, we have to accept that the press freedom myth is not working. It tells us more about the media of the past than the media of the present. And it does not provide any kind of compass to the future.

Conclusion

THE OLD ARGUMENTS for press freedom do not add up.

A free marketplace of ideas might sometimes lead to the truth, but it might just as well lead to a pack of lies. If you tell enough people that the earth is flat, then some of them will believe you. If you tell them that vaccinations cause autism, some of them will believe that, too. In fact, some people will believe pretty much anything; and most people will believe at least something that is not true. The truth does not emerge victorious from every encounter with falsehood. It is easily bruised.

The truth is more likely to prevail when people are obliged to be honest and discerning, to study the evidence and to listen to other arguments. This is what happens, on a good day, in scientific laboratories and courts of law. It is what happens when journalists live up to the ethical standards of their profession.

Since the early twentieth century, journalists have developed rules to guide their behaviour: to ensure the accuracy of what they publish, create space for alternative opinions and correct their mistakes. If all journalists followed these rules, then their audiences could be confident that they were at least pointing in the direction of truth (even if mistakes were made along the way, just as they are in science and law).

However, it only takes a few journalists to break these rules for audiences to lose their faith in journalism as a whole. Some audiences might wrongly place their trust in journalists who do not deserve that trust. Other audiences might wrongly mistrust journalists who are in fact trustworthy. One way or the other, the public will soon become cynical, and the entire field of journalism will suffer. This is what is happening now, as mischief-makers and autocrats shout 'fake news' at every critical report – no matter how accurate and important it may be. Journalism is losing its moral authority, not because *all* journalists are bad, but because *some* journalists are bad; and some bad people exploit that to discredit the whole profession – and so the public cannot easily tell the difference between the journalists who deserve our trust and those who do not.

The enemies of the media can attack it from the inside, as well as the outside. In the absence of ownership regulation, people with any kind of political, commercial and personal agenda can use media companies to advance their cause. This is happening in Hungary right now, where the associates of Viktor Orbán have bought up the country's newspapers and broadcasters in order to support the autocratic Prime Minister.[123] Even where independent media companies try to serve democracy, by publishing accurate journalism in the public interest, they are likely to have a certain perspective, and, in a democracy, audiences need to hear a range of views.

Journalists who are entirely free to express themselves

---

123 See Marius Dragomir, 'Central and Eastern Europe's Captured Media', *Project Syndicate*, 6 May 2019, available at https://www.project-syndicate.org/commentary/press-freedom-hungary-central-eastern-europe-by-marius-dragomir-2019-05.

may realise their potential as human beings, but they risk damaging the freedom and wellbeing of others. As John Stuart Mill told us, freedom is not absolute. We exist in a complex web of social relationships. When we cause harm to others, we tear this web, and we lose our right to absolute liberty.

Journalism is not the same as individual expression. It is a special kind of discourse that relies on rules that help journalists advance the truth, support democracy and avoid harming others. Journalism codes ask journalists to get their facts right, to be transparent about any conflicts of interest, and to respect the rights of others. Journalism that follows these rules is likely to serve the public interest. Journalism that breaks these rules is likely to harm the public interest.

At the start of this book, I asked whether there was a fundamental difference between the news media and social media. Should we regulate publishers or platforms? Publishers *and* platforms? *Neither* publishers *nor* platforms?

It is time to take a deep breath and accept that *all* forms of media have a responsibility to society. We all suffer the consequences of fake news, hate speech and covert propaganda, whether they appear in old media or new. We all need the media to be accountable for their impact. Sticks and stones may break our bones, but words can also cause us serious and irrevocable harm.

Does this mean that we need to reintroduce censorship – that we need the state to tell us what is and is not allowed?

No! We do not want the state getting directly involved in the business of journalism or social media. Unethical publishers and platforms may be troubling, but a repressive state poses a far greater threat. States have coercive powers at their disposal. They can lock us up, torture us and even kill us. Even where states do not use these powers, they can still exert a powerful chilling effect. Most people will avoid irritating the authorities if they fear that there is a prison cell somewhere in the background.

So is it deadlock, then? We cannot get what we need from an entirely free media, but we cannot expect the state to save us?

Not quite. Media freedom is not a zero-sum game.

We do not have to choose between perfect freedom or absolute repression. The state can support the conditions for a vibrant public sphere without exerting control over journalists or social media users. It can take steps to ensure that people have the opportunity to benefit from high-quality journalism in the public interest, and that people are free to use social media to express themselves and take part in democracy. At the same time, the state can protect people from harm, and limit the scope for abuse of media power.

Before anything else, however, the state must protect our fundamental human rights. These include the rights to freedom of expression, political participation and equal treatment before the law. Sometimes these rights come into conflict with each other. The human rights framework is a balancing act. It does not provide all the answers about freedom and responsibility, but it does at least pose the right questions. A state that does not respect human rights should have nothing whatsoever to do with the media. But a state that does respect human rights should follow five further principles in order to ensure a healthy public sphere.

Firstly, the state should set and enforce clear legal standards for all forms of expression – journalistic, individual, commercial and political. This does not mean that the state should censor us; but it does mean that the state should act to prevent us causing irrevocable harm to one another.

Law is not the same as censorship. Censors live in darkness. They exert covert pressure on journalists and publishers by reviewing publications before they see the light of day. When a censor blocks a piece of content, the public do not know what they have lost. By contrast, the law takes place in public. Whether it is civil (where we sue each other) or criminal (where the state prosecutes us), the law must be there, as a last resort, to protect us from harms such as defamation, harassment, invasion of privacy, hate speech, data theft, breach of copyright, false advertising and contempt of court. The law should be drawn narrowly – only where there is real evidence of harm – and used sparingly, and there should be a public interest exemption in all areas where journalists sometimes need to break the law, so long as they can show that it was necessary for them to do so.

There is a difference between, for example, publishing data that reveals the current location of soldiers or spies, and exposing corruption in defence spending. The law should be able to recognise this difference, and it should treat public interest journalism accordingly.

Secondly, the state should ensure that the law is accessible to everyone. In the United Kingdom, civil law is the preserve of the wealthy, and criminal law can be near-impossible to navigate in an era of reduced legal aid. States should guarantee access to justice, either through the courts or through some form of alternative dispute resolution such as mediation or arbitration. Regulators can also help with this, by enabling media companies and their users and audiences to resolve disputes quickly and straightforwardly.

Thirdly, the state must ensure that we all have access to public interest journalism. It should correct any market failures – for example, by breaking up media monopolies and encouraging the production of more diverse journalism. The state should consider subsidies and tax breaks where the news market does not meet the needs of society. It should structure any financial support to ensure that it is not influenced by political considerations but goes only to publishers with a demonstrable commitment to public interest journalism. In my view, the state should not seek to prevent the publication of unethical journalism, but it should create legal consequences for journalism that causes real harm; and it should create meaningful incentives for journalism that serves the public interest.

Fourthly, the state should ensure that we all have access to a form of social media that meets our needs. In the analogue world, the state has a duty to protect our right to assemble freely, even where this is disruptive – for example, when we park a boat on the street in a public protest. This duty should carry over into the digital world, where platforms provide an unparalleled opportunity for citizens to get together and raise awareness of challenging issues.

This means giving everyone the opportunity to get online if they want to. It may also mean intervening in the social media economy. For the time being, the market is giving us an abundance of opportunities to congregate online. But not all platforms are to everyone's taste.

Some have an intimidating culture of abuse. Some have a reputation for hoovering up our personal data. Just as we can choose where to be socially active in the offline world, so we should be able to choose a platform that suits us in the online world. Some of us like noisy pubs whilst others prefer a quiet cup of tea. If the market will not provide these options, then there may be a role for the state to step in.

Just as democratic states underwrite some form of public service broadcasting, so, in future, we may see new forms of public service social media – platforms that do not rely on advertising, and that do not therefore incentivise the most attention-grabbing and data-revealing forms of sharing. So long as we all have access to such a platform, we may be able to live without the most punitive forms of social media regulation. At the same time, the digital advertising market should be reformed, to ensure that consumers know how their data is being traded and when they are being sold propaganda. And, as with the news media, those who are responsible for the greatest harm should suffer real penalties – whether they are platform operators or users. There is no excuse for targeting people online because of their gender or the colour of their skin. Platforms that fail to tackle this form of abuse should come under increasing pressure.

Fifthly and finally, it is the state's job to help us become active media citizens. Whether we want to produce or consume media content, we are all players in the media economy. Journalists need special training, but audiences also need lessons in navigating the modern media. This is a complex and rapidly changing world, and the state cannot just abandon us to it. It needs to make sure that we know what we are doing, so that we can get the best out of our media and mitigate the worst.

The press freedom myth overstates the threats posed to the media by the state, and understates the threats posed to society by an absolutely free media. Conversely, it exaggerates the positive role played by the media and downplays the negative. We need to move away from this myth, with its Manichaean struggle between good and evil, and open the doors to a more pluralist approach. We need to set norms for the media, just as we do for other aspects of our lives: work, commerce, education, healthcare, construction and so on.

And then perhaps the media will truly help to advance the causes of truth, democracy and self-expression.

The opportunities here are at least as great as the challenges. We could use the power of the media to come together and solve the problems that face us and our beautiful planet. Or we could splinter into countless warring tribes, each with our own truths, unable to speak to each other, barely able even to *understand* each other. We have already travelled too far in that direction. It is time now to reset the relationship between the media and society; to take the best from the past and present and shape the media of the future.

At least, until the next technological revolution.

Acknowledgements

I AM GRATEFUL TO Yasmin Alibhai-Brown for commissioning this book, and to Olivia Beattie and her team at Biteback for publishing it with such attention to detail.

I am particularly grateful to Lisa Appignanesi, Rowan Cruft, Sir Harold Evans, Chris Frost, David Leigh, Alastair Niven, Fabienne Peter and Damian Tambini for reading and commenting on drafts of this book.

I am extremely lucky to work with a team of smart, dedicated and good-humoured people at IMPRESS. This book represents my own thinking and not IMPRESS policy, but I have benefited from numerous conversations and debates with my friends and colleagues, and I am extremely grateful to all of them.

I am also grateful to friends and former colleagues at

Cambridge University, *The Observer*, the Fabian Society, English PEN and the Sigrid Rausing Trust, with whom I began to shape the ideas that are set out in this book. I am particularly grateful to everybody who has disagreed with me. Milton was right about one thing: my truths have been sharpened by collision with yours. Nonetheless, all mistakes are my own.